Collaborative Innovation

Collaborative Innovation

How Clients and Service Providers
Can Work by Design to Achieve It

Tony Morgan

BEP BUSINESS EXPERT PRESS

Collaborative Innovation: How Clients and Service Providers Can Work by Design to Achieve It
Copyright © Business Expert Press, LLC, 2017.

First published in 2017 by
Business Expert Press, LLC
222 East 46th Street, New York, NY 10017
www.businessexpertpress.com

ISBN-13: 978-1-63157-631-7 (paperback)
ISBN-13: 978-1-63157-632-4 (e-book)

Business Expert Press Service Systems and Innovations in Business and Society Collection

Collection ISSN: 2326-2664 (print)
Collection ISSN: 2326-2699 (electronic)

Cover and interior design by S4Carlisle Publishing Services
Private Ltd., Chennai, India

First edition: 2017

10 9 8 7 6 5 4 3 2 1

Printed in the United States of America.

Abstract

Innovation can be a challenging subject. At its worst, it is a meaningless buzzword. At its best, it is a means of driving differentiating value for an organization. But how can innovation be consistently achieved in the context of a client–service provider relationship?

This publication provides a practical framework, with clear supporting recommendations, for clients and service providers to work together to overcome challenges and successfully manage, develop, and deliver innovation as a key part of their ongoing service relationship.

Real-world experience, guidance, and examples are provided to assist and enable organizations to gain additional value with their service partners through delivery of innovation *by design* rather than by accident.

Although targeted at service relationships between clients and external service providers, the content and recommendations are equally applicable and relevant for enterprises driving innovation internally or as part of a wider ecosystem.

Keywords

Innovation, Innovation Management, Collaboration, Service Innovation, Service, Services, Service Development, Service Delivery, Outsourcing, Sourcing, Partnership, Design, Procurement, Transition, Transformation.

Contents

Acknowledgments

There are many people I'd like to acknowledge and thank, whom I've worked with over the years, and who've provided positive support and advice, and in doing so influenced the contents of this publication. There are too many to list individually but I like to think you know who you are. I would specifically like to mention one person, Clive Harris. It was Clive who generated my interest in innovation and he has been a great mentor, inspiration, and friend to me and many others in IBM and beyond. Thank you, Clive. I hope you enjoy the book.

Preface

The contents of this publication are focused on understanding and overcoming challenges, which both clients and service providers face when attempting to manage, develop, and deliver innovation collaboratively as part of an ongoing service relationship.

The primary argument made is that when clients and service providers truly collaborate to drive innovation and do this *by design* rather than by accident, they can and do create higher value outcomes for both parties on a repeatable and sustainable basis, throughout the lifecycle of their service agreement and relationship.

Real-world experience, advice, guidance, and examples are provided for clients and service providers, to assist each to gain additional value from successful joint innovation with their service partners.

The objective is to provide a practical framework, with clear supporting recommendations, for achieving successful outcomes through joint innovation *by design*. Although targeted at service relationships between clients and external service providers, the content and recommendations are equally applicable and relevant for enterprises driving innovation internally or as part of a wider ecosystem.

CHAPTER 1

Introduction

Introducing Collaborative Innovation *by Design*

The contents of this publication are focused on understanding and overcoming challenges, which both client and service providers face, when attempting to manage, develop, and deliver innovation collaboratively as part of an ongoing service relationship.

The primary argument made is that when clients and service providers truly collaborate to drive innovation and do this *by design* rather than by accident, they can and do create higher value outcomes for both parties on a repeatable and sustainable basis, throughout the life cycle of their service agreement and relationship.

Real-world experience, advice, guidance, and examples are provided for clients and service providers, assisting each to gain additional value from successful joint innovation with their service partners.

The objective is to provide a practical framework, with clear supporting recommendations, for achieving successful outcomes through joint innovation *by design*.

Although targeted at service relationships between clients and external service providers, the majority of the content and recommendations are equally applicable for use in internal service arrangements, where the client is a business unit, function, or team within an organization and the service provider is a different business unit, function, or team within the same organization. The challenges faced in such a situation are often the same as in an internal client and external service provider scenario.

A Little on Terminology

I thought it useful to include at the very beginning a brief explanation and introduction to some of the key terminology used in the context of the publication's content. Many people will be very familiar with some or all of the terminology used, while others may not be. From experience, different words and phrases are often used when describing the same thing in the areas covered. A common understanding of terminology is important, between the author and reader and, more importantly, between clients and service providers.

It is almost business as usual for one organization to use a word or phrase to describe something while another uses an alternative, and this frequently leads to confusion, misunderstanding, and sometimes even mistrust. In a service relationship, it's frequently a good idea for a "client" and "service provider" to agree written definitions for key terminology and if and when needed refer back to these, not just in terms of a contract but, equally importantly, to support the practical day-to-day working of people on the ground using, delivering, and supporting services.

Innovation—a thorny one to start with; as outlined in the following chapters, innovation can mean many different things in different contexts to different people and organizations, but for general purposes in the context of this publication, innovation refers to the use of new ideas, or existing ideas in a new context, to drive change that delivers value.

Types of innovation—there are many ways to define and describe innovation:

- One traditional view of the types of innovation is as follows:
  - **New product and service development innovation**—creation of new or improvement of existing products or services
  - **Operational innovation**—improvement of existing business processes
  - **Business model innovation**—changes to organizational and business models
- A second, more recent, view of innovation includes the following:
  - **Core innovation**—improvements in existing business products and services, operations, and business models for existing customers and markets

- ○ **Adjacent innovation**—expansion into new business products and services and/or markets, in areas linked to existing core business
- ○ **Transformational innovation**—expansion into totally new business products and services and/or markets, in totally new areas not linked to the existing core business
- A third view looks at the level of innovation, which can span all the way from:
  - ○ **Incremental innovation**—minor or marginal changes and improvement to existing products and services, operations, and/or business models
  - ○ **Disruptive innovation**—creation of new-to-the-world products, services, and business models that create new markets and industries and/or disrupt existing ones

Open innovation—in simplistic terms in the context of this publication is when organizations reach out and make use of external ideas, capabilities, and routes to market, in addition to internal ones.

Client—customer organization/end user organization/organization that uses the services of a supplier or service provider.

Service provider—organization that supplies specific (usually contracted) services to one or more client organizations (i.e., in the context of this book, the same as supplier below).

Supplier—organization that supplies specific (usually contracted) services to one or more client organizations (i.e., in the context of this book, the same as service provider above).

Service (or Service offering)—a means by which a service provider delivers value to a client organization by facilitating outcomes the client wishes to achieve, as part of a joint agreement.

Service improvement—improvements to increase the efficiency, maximize effectiveness, and optimize the cost of services and underlying service management processes. Don't worry, we'll return to this subject and ask the sometimes thorny question: "Is service improvement innovation?"

Engagement phase—process through which a client organization defines its requirements for one or more services and selects and contracts with a service provider to provide them.

Transformation phase—change program (typically in early stages of a services contract) where the service provider works with the client organization to deliver changes to enable enhanced ongoing run of service(s).

Run phase—sometimes known as business as usual—ongoing delivery and management of service(s) provided by the service provider to the client organization.

What Is the Problem We Are Looking to Address?

The core of the issue that led to this publication is that innovation is difficult to achieve and maintain, particularly in the context of an ongoing client–service provider relationship. In many ways, achieving successful innovation between a client and a service provider, as part of a service relationship, should be little different to the situation where any two organizations make a conscious decision to pool capabilities and do something new or different that will drive value for both parties.

Much research and practical implementation has been done to extend Henry Chesbrough's original work and analysis on inside-out and outside-in aspects of "open innovation." The focus of this publication is really on one specific aspect or angle of open innovation, that is, innovation between two organizations that already have a service-based relationship but often, wider inputs and elements of open innovation will be involved. It's a fascinating area and one that virtually all forward-thinking organizations are considering to some extent.

We know from experience there can be challenges. With elements of open innovation, there always are, but these are now widely understood and can be managed effectively to enable success. Things are never quite this simple, though, are they? Innovation can be a much-bandied buzzword, put around by service providers, with little substance to back it up. Frequently, clients may ask for innovation from their service providers, without really understanding what it is or what they want. Little surprise, then, innovation is a word and an area where mistrust and misunderstandings often exist between clients and service providers. In many cases, it is the category where clients rate their service providers lowest in terms of formal client satisfaction and value derived from the overall relationship with the service provider.

In addition, it is an area where service providers can be exasperated by their clients.

There is no doubt that dissatisfied clients and frustrated service providers exist, each with their own war stories to tell. However, innovation between clients and service providers definitely does happen. There are great examples of this across many industries, but in the past, this has often occurred as much by accident as *by design*. This, in itself, can cause very good results, but accidental innovation is unlikely to be consistent or sustainable.

The reality is innovation between clients and service providers is difficult to achieve and equally challenging to sustain, but there is a positive side. In this publication, we make the case that when clients and suppliers do truly collaborate to drive innovation and do this *by design* rather than by accident, they can and do create higher value outcomes for both parties on a repeatable and ongoing basis, throughout the life cycle of their service agreement and relationship.

The book includes a number of recommendations, approaches, and techniques for achieving this. The author readily admits that the content is not based on rocket science but all too often some or many of the challenges described in the following chapters exist, with no concerted plan to address them. If this is not the case in your organization, I'm very pleased and would love to know if you've already adopted some of the approaches recommended in this publication and/or have made use of equally effective alternative approaches. One of my experiences of working on joint innovation between clients and service providers is there is always something new to learn.

Much of what I've looked to build into this publication is derived from my own direct real-world experience of managing, developing, and delivering innovation between clients and service providers in the IT services industry. The rest comes from extensive discussion and collaboration with others, including chairing and facilitating cross-industry groups, workshops, and debates on the topic. I firmly believe the challenges outlined exist generically in many industries, and so hope the content will be useful for a wide range of organizations as they look to create new relationships between client and service provider organizations or build upon and improve existing ones.

Lastly, this book is about innovation, and so it can't just be about looking back and taking lessons learned from experiences, good and bad.

Thankfully, there will always be new things to learn, different ways to do things, and improvements to make. The book also highlights some of the newer areas that are making a real difference in the effectiveness of collaborative client–supplier innovation. Of course, there will be others, and next year there will be different ones again, and so on. The author would love to engage with the readers on their thoughts, lessons learned, and new approaches, on an ongoing basis, so please do get in touch.

The Author's Experience

My career in IT and technology services began in 1987 after leaving university, when I worked in the internal IT business unit of a number of client organizations. Since joining IBM in 1998, one of the major reasons I've enjoyed myself and been able to keep myself motivated has been the ability to find new and interesting roles every few years. Having been Chief Architect for IBM on multiple large client engagements and ongoing service contracts a number of years ago, I made a slightly sideways move into Service Innovation–related roles.

My interest started when I attended an IBM technical leaders conference. One of the speakers gave a fascinating talk on the work he was carrying out as IBM Innovation Leader for a very large IT services and sourcing contract with a major global financial services client. In this role, he was working alongside an opposite number in the client in something called a Value Creation Centre, which was a joint team managing a portfolio of innovation-related activities, rather than a physical place.

In effect, this was a joint investment between the financial services company, as the client, and IBM, as the service provider, focused on areas where the client organization could use technology to do something new or different to drive business value. The concept included developing opportunities for innovation by focusing on the client's business challenges and opportunities; utilizing the client's business knowledge and capabilities, and IBM and partner industry and technology capabilities; developing these and ultimately delivering them; and also measuring the value derived.

As I listened avidly to this presentation, I thought this was exactly what IBM and other service providers should be doing with their clients but often were not. I was delighted when the speaker said he was looking to expand his team, and connected with him afterward. Before long, I applied for and got the role of Innovation Architect, working in the Value Creation Centre team. What I didn't quite realize at the time was I was part of the Innovation Leader's "exit plan" from the account, that is, he'd been looking to recruit somebody who could quickly take on his Innovation leadership role. So before long I was the Innovation Leader of this large Value Creation Centre. In parallel, the previous Innovation Leader became a long-term colleague, friend and mentor and has had a hugely positive and supportive influence on my career ever since.

This was a job I loved. I learned many positive and valuable lessons, a number of which were vital for my subsequent roles and have been incorporated into the chapters of this book. Both organizations were committed to the success of the innovation partnership, there was strong and engaged sponsorship, there were great connections between business and technology, and strong teams on both sides committed to working together to drive innovation and real business value for the client organization and benefits for IBM too (more on that later).

After this role, my next move within IBM was to join a small team developing a new innovation program for a cross-industry portfolio of IT service and sourcing clients in the United Kingdom and Ireland. Again, I quickly became the leader of this team, and for the next four years I worked with clients and IBM teams in my own business unit and across the depth and breadth of IBM to partner with our clients on a huge range of innovation-related activities, from one-off innovation workshops to specific innovation-related projects to ongoing joint innovation programs.

In this role, my job title was IBM Global Technology Services (my business unit) Client Chief Innovation Officer. The "Client" word is important. My role was not to work on internal IBM facing innovations, which were obviously also hugely important, but to drive joint innovation between IBM service account teams and our clients.

Leading a small central innovation team, my role was really split into two parts.

1. Working directly with clients: I worked with a number of specifically targeted clients to manage, develop, and deliver joint innovation—running innovation workshops, developing and delivering a range

of innovation projects, and supporting the establishment and governance of joint innovation programs.

2. Enabling IBM teams: Working with IBM engagement, account, and service teams to skill them in managing, developing, and delivering joint innovation proactively with their own clients; developing repeatable innovation-related assets; enabling enhanced access to wider IBM innovation programs and resources; creating positive communications of success stories; and creating a buzz around innovation within IBM and our clients.

The first part of the role was very important for me personally, as working with clients is where I get a large part of my job satisfaction. The second aspect was critical to the success of the role. We had a small central innovation team but the potential to have a much greater impact if every client account team proactively engaged their client to manage, develop, and deliver joint innovation and had the know-how and capability to do it.

For four years, it was an absolute pleasure and privilege to work with so many fantastic people in our clients and in IBM and partner organizations. I learned a huge amount, often through success but sometimes, it has to be admitted, through challenges and even failures. Again, I have looked to embed this experience into the learning and recommendations in the following chapters.

During and after the role, I worked with IBM services and wider client facing teams across Europe and beyond to learn from them and cascade learning from the experience of the successful client innovation program in the United Kingdom and Ireland. One aspect of this was to work with a small team of great people to develop a new global IBM Leaders "Master Class," focused on collaborative innovation with clients. This is now taught to senior client facing IBM professionals across the globe, and I've personally trained teams across Europe and in the United States and China, learning a great deal about the value and importance of geography-based cultures along the way.

It is important to see outside your own little world, even if it is big and blue. My favorite open innovation–related quote is the one from Bill Joy, cofounder of Sun Microsystems: "Because not all the smart people work for you." With this in mind, I reached outside IBM to engage with and learn from others. I led the Special Interest Group for Innovation in the UK National Outsourcing Association (now known as the Global Sourcing Association) for a number of years, leading research, discussion, and workshops with clients, suppliers, and third-party advisers. The insights gained have also helped give me a wider perspective and see the common patterns and challenges facing a much wider group of clients and service providers. Once more, I've striven to bring this learning into the contents of this publication.

In recent years, my focus has included working with university students and universities on innovation-related topics. A number of times in this publication I make reference to IBM's Extreme Blue innovation program. This is a program that assigns student interns to work, supported by experienced IBMers, on client challenges to create new-to-the-world capabilities. I've been a lead mentor for a number of Extreme Blue projects, and the IBM teams, clients, and I have never ceased to be amazed by the brilliant solutions developed by the students.

Inspired by my interaction with these teams, I've become involved with a number of universities in the United Kingdom, in particular the University of Leeds, whose focus on the importance of innovation management has impressed me. This has included supporting the development and teaching of a new student module, Innovation Management in Practice, where I was given the challenge—"If a student becomes an innovation manager, what should they do when they arrive for work on Monday morning?" This work has been very rewarding. I was delighted in 2016 when I was appointed by the Royal Academy of Engineering as Visiting Professor of Innovation in Industry at the University of Leeds, which I am fitting alongside my day job as I think the experience benefits myself, my employer, and our clients. There is a particular focus in this role on improving the employability of students, particularly engineering students, and my focus includes assisting the students to understand and develop the T- and TT-shaped skills profiles, which I believe are critical for the development and delivery of innovation success. More on this when we discuss the role of the Innovation Leader.

Let me stop blowing my trumpet for a moment, even if the reason for doing it is to demonstrate the real-world experiences upon which this publication is built. I would like to admit a truth. Despite the effort of many people across IBM, we have not yet successfully convinced every IT services and sourcing client the value of jointly collaborating with IBM as a service provider on innovation. There are a minority of clients who, for a number of reasons, are still reticent to focus on collaborative innovation, or believe that all the effort to deliver innovation should come from the service provider alone (an approach I believe will simply not work).

In recent times, we've increasingly looked at things from the client viewpoint. The use of Design Thinking–related techniques and approaches is hugely beneficial here. Empathy is very important. If the client team does not recognize the value or wish to input into innovation activity, there must be a reason for this. Design Thinking and additional actions have assisted moving things forward with a good number of these clients, but not yet all. I'm sure this is true for many service providers. It would be interesting to get such clients to review and feedback on the contents of this publication. In the chapter centered on Client Challenges, I've attempted to consider the world empathetically from a client's point of view, an important consideration for all service providers. I hope this works.

Overall, the innovation program has been a significant success. Many clients have derived significant value and business benefits from our joint innovation activities, and the additional investment and focus on innovation from the IBM team has been very good for IBM too. We were tasked with developing and delivering a program of joint innovation with our clients that would deliver business benefits to the clients, increase the value they gained from their service relationship with IBM, improve formal client satisfaction, and (yes, let's be honest about this) drive additional business for IBM. We achieved all these things.

Over the four years, our formal client satisfaction scores for innovation rose steadily and significantly, as we learned and improved. We reached a good place and a key target, with more than 80 percent of the IT services and sourcing clients covered by the program rating IBM 8 out of 10 or above for innovation. The current team is driving to improve this further still, using new and emerging capabilities and approaches, as they should. But it was not like that at the beginning. There was much to do and there were many improvements to make. Many people did a lot of very good things, and the IBM team and our clients learned many lessons along the way, which I look to share with you in the following chapters.

CHAPTER 2

Client Challenges

Key Client Challenges

This chapter focuses on the challenges faced by client organizations in managing, developing, and delivering collaborative innovation with their service providers. Of course, not all client organizations will have all the challenges listed, but the majority of client organizations are likely to be facing at least a number of them, either at the current time or at some point in the future. Experience-based recommendations for overcoming such challenges are included in the following chapters.

Many people working in client organizations will instantly recognize many of the items listed. Others may be less obviously recognizable. Many of the items may raise a few eyebrows with some people. These items may not even be perceived as challenges from the client perspective, but all of the items described have been included as the author believes they pose real barriers to successful collaborative innovation.

The client challenges have been categorized as follows:

- Time, resources, and funding
- Sponsorship and leadership
- Innovation understanding
- Service provider–related challenges
- Culture and motivation

Client Challenges

Time, Resources, and Funding	Sponsorship and Leadership	Innovation Understanding	Service Provider-Related Challenges	Culture and Motivation

The challenges, as I see them, are outlined in more detail in the following subsections. For some excellent additional perspectives beyond this publication, recommended reading includes *Reaching the Goal: How Managers Improve Service Businesses* by John Ricketts and *Can Two Rights Make a Wrong: Insights from IBM's Tangible Culture Project* by Sarah Moulton Reger.

Time, Resources, and Funding

Some of the biggest challenges for organizations considering use of a structured approach for managing, developing, and delivering innovation are the availability of time, resources, and funding to focus on applying innovation to their business challenges and opportunities. This is as true for an organization looking to drive innovation purely internally as for a client looking to drive innovation in collaboration with its service providers.

This is, of course, a classic innovation conundrum—we don't have time to sharpen the saw because we're too busy cutting down trees with a blunt saw, or, to put it another way from a client perspective, we don't have time to focus on innovation this year because we already have a full book of change projects to run and some of them aren't going as well as we'd hoped.

I've spent time working with a number of client organizations in this position. Representatives from such companies have sometimes told me they love the idea of taking a structured approach to innovation within their own business and are equally keen to work in collaboration with their service providers to develop and deliver innovation but this will have to wait until next year (or the year after and so on).

Specific challenges for client organizations in this area include the following:

- "We don't have time to focus on innovation because we have a full change program"
- "We can't focus on innovation at the moment because the people and other resources we've got are already fully committed to run the business and change the business activities"

- "We can't focus on innovation at the moment because our budget is already fully committed to meet the costs required to run the business and on delivering already approved change the business activities"

When these challenges are encountered, it will be important for the client to take a step back and discuss internally, and with their service providers, how innovation could be applied *by design*, at least at the outset, to address challenges in the current service and change program, for example, to improve quality or efficiency of service and/or change activities to reduce costs. Savings achieved, or a proportion of them, can then be reapplied to higher value change the business innovation activities. These can drive further value for the client and offer business opportunities for the service provider, perhaps offset against reduced revenues from core services, due to the impact of implemented efficiency-focused service improvement innovations.

An additional consideration for client organizations is to review the value of potential innovation activities against activities planned within current budget allocations. An example of this is included in the Proof Points chapter, where a client determined to reallocate an element of budget from previously planned change activity to deliver specific items identified and developed during joint innovation activity with a service provider, on the basis of the higher value generated from the innovation project, compared to existing budgeted change activities

Sponsorship and Leadership

It is possible to drive innovation successfully from the shop floor, in a skunk works type mode, without executive or management support and sponsorship, but the value derived from such an approach is likely to be limited and unsustainable.

At times, organizations talk about making innovation a priority, at an executive level, but do not place any substance behind such a statement. This can be particularly damaging to the people within the organization and the employees of partner, supplier, and service provider organizations, because the word innovation, itself, loses credibility and is seen simply as a buzzword rather than as anything meaningful.

From experience, there is generally no shortage of ideas for doing new things or improving existing things in the vast majority of organizations, but a key challenge is how best to approach the sponsorship and leadership from the top required to foster innovation and the supporting organization's, processes, and capabilities required to successfully manage, develop, and deliver innovation across all levels of the organization.

Specific challenges for client organizations in this area include the following:

- "We have no executive or management support for developing and delivering innovation in the overall business and/or in our business unit."
- "Nobody is responsible for developing and delivering innovation in our overall business and/or in our business unit."
- "Nobody is responsible for developing and delivering innovation in collaboration with our service provider(s)."

It will not be enough for client executives to state that innovation is an important priority. They will also need to put in place the tangible organization, process, and funding enablers covered in later chapters needed to encourage an innovation culture in their own organization and in the service provider's organization. Empowered leadership will be needed to work with each service provider to input into a joint innovation management and execution approach. This can include idea generation and identification, idea review and prioritization, capability and business case development, sponsorship and funding for later stage innovation activity, delivery and commercialization of the innovation, in order for tangible value to be derived and the benefits measured.

Innovation Understanding

Another challenge for many organizations when considering driving a structured approach to managing, developing, and delivering innovation is understanding what innovation really means in the context of their own business or business unit and in the context of their relationship with their service providers.

Innovation is a word that means many different things to different people. The same organization may have quite different views on innovation across their business units. In addition, as outlined in the Terminology section of the Introduction, there are many different types of innovation. Some people may view innovation as being purely related to new product and service development or about application of the latest technology. Others may wish to focus innovation efforts on a series of small, incremental improvements to existing operations. Equally, a different group may dismiss such incremental change as not being innovation at all and see innovation as purely focusing on disruptive or transformative change.

If a client doesn't work with its service providers to agree what innovation is in the context of their service relationships, how will the service provider know how to deliver it, and how will the client know they are getting or not getting it?

Specific challenges for client organizations in this area include the following:

- "We don't have an understanding of what innovation really means to the wider business."
- "We don't know what innovation means for our business unit."
- "We don't have a level of agreement with our service provider(s) of what we want from them or what they mean by innovation." (Note the duplication with the next subsection.)

There are no right or wrong answers here in terms of what the definition of innovation should be. The key, as described in the following chapters, is for the client and service provider to get together and jointly agree, define, focus on, and measure what innovation means in the context of their relationship.

Service Provider–Related Challenges

Having spent the majority of my career, working for a service provider organization, I write this subsection with a little trepidation, but the truth will out. One of the specific challenges client organizations can have in collaborative relationships with their service provider(s) is the level of understanding and capability of their service providers in the context of innovation.

Just as the client organization can have internal challenges around the sponsorship, leadership, and understanding of innovation, their service provider(s) may well be in the same boat. Some service providers may talk up innovation as a priority and state they have innovative capabilities but then have not sufficient substance to back up their claims. There may not be sufficient sponsorship, leadership, process, and/or capability within the service provider's organization to make true collaborative innovation with their client(s) work. In addition, the service provider may harbor very different views of what innovation is to their clients.

Equally, the service provider must put the basics in place for the client to earn the right to even have an innovation conversation. The basics include solid service and change delivery. Finally, the relationship between the client and service provider will be a critical enabler for innovation. If this is broken, it is unlikely either organization will focus on or derive value from collaborative innovation.

Some of the specific challenges for client organizations in this area are as follows:

- "There is no executive or management support for developing and delivering innovation in our service provider(s)."
- "Nobody is responsible for developing and delivering innovation in collaboration with us in our service provider(s)."
- "We don't have a level of agreement with our service provider(s) of what we want from them or what they mean by innovation." (Note the duplication with previous subsection.)
- "Our service provider(s) are not providing a quality service, so why would we wish to develop an innovation agenda with them?"
- "Our relationship with our service provider(s) is not strong enough for us to wish to develop collaborative innovation with them."

As detailed in later chapters, it will be key for the client to consider the innovation capabilities, motivations, and proof points of potential service providers during the Pre-engagement phase planning and during the Engagement phase of the service life cycle. If innovation is a priority for the client organization, then the innovation capabilities of potential service providers should be part of the selection criteria for choosing a service provider.

If the service provider is not providing a robust quality of service, it is unlikely the client organization will even consider a wider innovation agenda. In this case, it is down to the service provider, supported by the client organization where appropriate, to apply innovation to improve service quality. Understandably, many clients will not consider this as innovation but simply the service provider doing what they should have done in the first place. However, once the service is robust, many clients will then be willing to engage their service providers on a wider scope innovation agenda.

Culture and Motivation

To some, this may appear a less tangible area for client challenges than the others, but it is of critical importance. If the culture of an organization does not support and enable its employees to focus on innovation and/ or if the employees are not motivated to drive innovation with their service provider(s), then it is unlikely to happen. There is a strong link and dependency here to the Sponsorship and Leadership subsection above.

A further consequence may be those employees who really do wish to raise new ideas and develop and deliver innovation will be turned off by the lack of an innovation culture and/or the lack of motivation within their colleagues. Once this happens, the productivity of such staff is likely to fall, and in the long term they are likely to look elsewhere within the wider organization or beyond to find a role that better meets their needs.

Specific challenges for client organizations in this area include the following:

- "Our organization does not value innovation, so why should we bother?"
- "Innovation is something the service provider will do for us or to us, so we don't need to do anything."

One aspect of culture and motivation is the level of proactivity in the client to understand what is most important to their business and to communicate this to the service provider, in order to be able to focus innovation on targeted areas and themes that will drive most value, rather than adopt a scattergun approach, and to provide support and input during innovation-related activities. Innovation in a service relationship is not done to the client; it is achieved in partnership with the service provider.

Equally, the service provider must be proactive when working with the client to find out what is most important to the client and determine where the service provider's capabilities can be applied to deliver most value to the client's business through innovation.

Successful innovation in a collaborative client–service provider relationship is more likely to be achieved when the culture in both organizations is similarly supportive of making innovation happen *by design* rather than by accident, but much more on this later.

CHAPTER 3

Service Provider Challenges

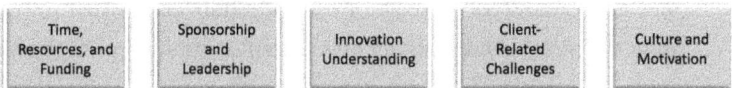

Key Service Provider Challenges

This chapter focuses on the challenges faced by service provider organizations in managing, developing, and delivering collaborative innovation with their clients. Of course, not all service provider organizations will have all the challenges listed, but the majority of organizations are likely to be facing at least a number of them, either at the current time or at some point in the future. Experience-based recommendations for overcoming such challenges are included in the following chapters.

Many people working in service provider organizations will instantly recognize many of the items listed. Others may be less obviously recognizable. Many of the items may raise a few eyebrows with some people. These items may not even be perceived as challenges from the service provider perspective, but all of the items described have been included as the author believes they pose real barriers to successful collaborative innovation.

The service provider challenges have been categorized as follows:

- Time, resources, and funding
- Sponsorship and leadership
- Innovation understanding
- Client-related challenges
- Culture and motivation

Service Provider Challenges

| Time, Resources, and Funding | Sponsorship and Leadership | Innovation Understanding | Client-Related Challenges | Culture and Motivation |

The challenges, as I see them, are outlined in more detail in the following subsections. For some excellent additional perspectives beyond this publication, recommended reading includes *Reaching the Goal: How Managers Improve Service Businesses* by John Ricketts and *Can Two Rights Make a Wrong: Insights from IBM's Tangible Culture Project* by Sarah Moulton Reger.

Time, Resources, and Funding

Some of the biggest challenges for organizations considering to use a structured approach for managing, developing, and delivering innovation are the availability of time, resources, and funding to focus on applying innovation to their business challenges and opportunities. This is as true for an organization looking to drive innovation purely internally as for a service provider looking to drive innovation in collaboration with its clients.

This, of course, is a classic innovation conundrum—we don't have time to sharpen the saw because we're too busy cutting down trees with a blunt saw, or, to put it another way from a service provider perspective, we don't have time to focus on innovation this year because we have to run the service, we have committed change projects and activities to deliver, and we may already have a number of issues.

I've discussed issues in this area with a number of service providers and service provider account teams. Representatives from such organizations have sometimes told me they love the idea of taking a structured approach to innovation in collaboration with their clients to develop and deliver innovation, but this will have to wait until next year (or the year after and so on).

Specific challenges for service provider organizations in this area include the following:

- "We don't have time to focus on innovation because we have to run the service."
- "We can't focus on innovation at the moment because the people and other resources we've got are already fully committed to running the service and working on existing committed change projects and activities."

- "We can't focus on innovation at the moment because our budget is already fully committed to running the service and existing planned change projects and activities."

When these challenges are encountered, it will be important for the service provider to take a step back and discuss internally, and with their client, how innovation could be applied *by design*, at least at the outset, to address challenges in the current service and change program. For example, innovation could be used to focus on improving the quality or efficiency of the service and/or change activities to reduce costs. Savings achieved, or a proportion of them, can then be reapplied to higher value change the business innovations. These can drive further value for the client and offer business opportunities for the service provider, perhaps offset against reduced revenues from core services, if the service provider has agreed to share the cost benefits of the impact of implemented efficiency-focused service improvement innovations.

An additional consideration for service provider organizations is to review the value of potential innovation activities against activities planned within current budget allocations. If greater potential value for the client and service provider can be identified from proposed innovation activities in comparison to already agreed change items, there will be a strong case for agreement, if appropriate, to reallocate funds to focus on development and delivery of the innovation activities.

Sponsorship and Leadership

It is possible to drive innovation successfully from the shop floor, in a skunk works type mode, without executive or management support and sponsorship, but the value derived from such an approach is likely to be limited and unsustainable.

At times, organizations talk about making innovation a priority, at an executive level, but do not place any substance behind such a statement. This can be particularly damaging to the people within the organization and the employees of partner, supplier, and client organizations, because the word innovation, itself, loses credibility and is seen simply as a buzzword, rather than as anything meaningful.

From experience, there is generally no shortage of ideas for doing new things or improving existing things in the vast majority of organizations, but a key challenge is how best to approach the sponsorship and leadership from the top required to foster innovation and the supporting organizations, processes, and capabilities required to successfully manage, develop, and deliver innovation across all levels of the organization.

Specific challenges for service provider organizations in this area include the following:

- "We have no executive or management support for developing and delivering innovation in the overall business and/or in our service business unit and/or account team."
- "Nobody is responsible for developing and delivering innovation in our overall business and/or in our service business unit and/or account team."
- "Nobody is responsible for developing and delivering innovation in collaboration with our clients."

It will not be enough for service provider executives to state that innovation is an important priority. They will also need to put in place the tangible organization, process, and funding enablers covered in later chapters needed to encourage an innovation culture in their own organization and in the client's organization. Empowered leadership will be needed to work with each client to input into a joint innovation management and execution approach. This can include idea generation and identification, idea review and prioritization, capability and business case development, sponsorship and funding for later stage innovation activity, delivery and commercialization of the innovation, in order for tangible value to be derived and the benefits measured.

Innovation Understanding

Another challenge for many organizations when considering driving a structured approach to managing, developing, and delivering innovation is understanding what innovation means in the context of their own business or business unit and in the context of their relationship with their clients.

Innovation is a word that means many different things to different people. The same organization may have quite different views on innovation across their business units. In addition, as outlined in the Terminology section of the Introduction, there are many different types of innovation. Some people within the service provider may view innovation as being purely related to new service development or about application of the latest technology. Others may wish to focus innovation efforts on a series of small, incremental improvements to the existing service. Equally, a different group may dismiss such incremental change as not being innovation at all and see innovation as purely focusing on the initial transition and transformation phase of the relationship or contract.

If a service provider doesn't work with each client to agree what innovation is in the context of their service relationship, how will the service provider know how to deliver it, and how will the client know they are getting or not getting it?

Specific challenges for service provider organizations in this area include the following:

- "We don't know what innovation means in the context of delivering innovation to our clients in general."
- "We don't have a level of agreement with our client(s) what they want from or they mean by innovation." (Note the duplication with the next subsection.)

There are no right or wrong answers in terms of what the definition of innovation should be here. The key, as described in the following chapters, is for the client and service provider to get together and jointly agree, define, focus on, and measure what innovation means in the context of their relationship.

Client-Related Challenges

Just as the service provider organization can have internal challenges around the sponsorship, leadership, and understanding of innovation, their clients(s) may well be in the same boat. Some clients may talk up their need for innovation but then not sufficient substance to enable it to be delivered for and with them. There may not be sufficient sponsorship, leadership, process, and/or capability within the client's organization to make true collaborative innovation with their service provider(s) work. In addition, the client may harbor very different views of what innovation is to their clients.

Finally, the relationship between the client and service provider will be a critical enabler for innovation. If this is broken, it is unlikely either organization will focus on or drive value from collaborative innovation.

Some of the specific challenges for service provider organizations in this area are as follows:

- "There is no executive or management support for developing and delivering innovation in our client(s)."
- "Nobody is responsible for developing and delivering innovation in collaboration with us in our clients)."
- "We don't have a level of agreement with our clients(s) what they want from or they mean by innovation." (Duplicate with previous subsection.)
- "Our relationship with our client(s) is not strong enough for us to wish to develop collaborative innovation with them."

For service providers who do possess real innovation capabilities, this can be one of the most frustrating challenge areas. On some occasions, the service provider can be chomping at the bit to manage, develop, and deliver innovation for the client, but be frustrated by the client's lack of understanding of and/or motivation for joint innovation. In this case, if the service provider is delivering a quality service and has a solid relationship with the client, they can engage with the client to highlight the potential benefits in this area, particularly highlighting proof points with other clients and the business benefits such clients have received from a joint focus on innovation *by design*. From experience, many clients will get this and embryonic innovation activity can begin, with a focus on quick-win innovation activities to demonstrate the value.

If the relationship is not strong and/or the client is not receptive to a joint focus on innovation, there is realistically only so much a service provider can do. With selected clients, it will be better to focus on core service and change delivery and target resources and investments into joint innovation with other clients in the portfolio.

Culture and Motivation

To some, this may appear a less tangible area for client challenges than the others, but it is of critical importance. If the culture of an organization does not support and enable its employees to focus on innovation and/ or if the employees are not motivated to drive innovation with their service provider(s), then it is unlikely to happen. There is a strong link and dependency here to the Sponsorship and Leadership subsection above.

A further consequence may be those employees who really do wish to raise new ideas and develop and deliver innovation will be turned off by the lack of an innovation culture and/or the lack of motivation within their colleagues. Once this happens, the productivity of such staff is likely to fall, and in the long term they are likely to look elsewhere within the wider organization or beyond to find a role that better meets their needs.

Specific challenges for service provider organizations in this area include the following:

- "Our organisation does not value innovation, so why should we bother?"
- "The client does not value innovation, so why should we bother?"
- "Innovation is something the client expects to happen without their active participation."

One aspect of culture and motivation is the level of proactivity in the service provider to understand what is most important to the client and determine where the service provider's capabilities can be applied to deliver most value to the client's business through innovation.

Equally, the client must be proactive when working with the service provider to understand what is most important to their business and communicate this to the service provider, and to provide support and input during innovation-related activities. Innovation in a service relationship is not done to the client, it is achieved in partnership with the service provider.

Successful innovation in a collaborative client–service provider relationship is more likely to be achieved when the culture in both organizations is similarly supportive of making innovation happen *by design,* rather than by accident, but much more on this later.

CHAPTER 4

Service Relationship Considerations

Why Is a Service Relationship Different?

This publication opened by stating that in many ways achieving successful innovation between a client and service provider as part of a service relationship should be little different to any two organizations who make a conscious decision to pool capabilities and do something new or different to drive value for both parties. While this is true, there are a number of key considerations that need to be taken into account in terms of the particular context and nuances of a service relationship, which come with a balance of advantages and disadvantages.

This chapter describes a number of these key considerations, which should be carefully considered when developing innovation *by design* as part of a client and service provider relationship.

The items covered are as follows:

- Service improvement versus innovation
- Life-cycle considerations
- Contractual considerations
- Commercial considerations
- Intellectual property considerations
- Mutual knowledge and understanding

Service Relationship Nuances

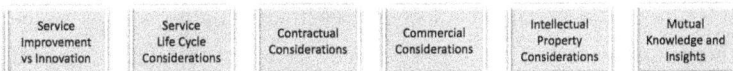

| Service Improvement vs Innovation | Service Life Cycle Considerations | Contractual Considerations | Commercial Considerations | Intellectual Property Considerations | Mutual Knowledge and Insights |

Service Improvement versus Innovation

One question I've often been asked in a service relationship context is when is it something innovation and when is it plain old-fashioned service improvement? Often the two coincide. A strong ongoing service improvement program can be a great source of a series of incremental improvements, using new or existing ideas that result in change that delivers value, in terms of increased efficiency, lower cost, higher levels of service quality or availability, and so on.

In the wider context of the innovation word, to me, this definitely is innovation and when combined together a set of marginal improvements can make a significant overall improvement. Consider the Sky and Great Britain cycling teams, who achieved huge success through a concerted focus on driving a relatively large number of incremental improvement marginal gain–based innovations. This is very much an example of innovation *by design*.

In terms of the context of a client–service provider relationship, my view on whether service improvement is innovation is "it depends on the view of the client". As we shall see in the next chapter, the client and service provider should agree a definition, scope, and focus areas for their joint innovation activity.

Some clients will consider service improvement as the area where all innovation efforts should be focused. Others will wish to focus on a combination of service improvements and wider scope innovations for their business unit or wider organization. Another set of clients will state that service improvement is not innovation at all in their eyes - it is business as usual. To these clients, innovation activity should be focused elsewhere and service improvement should simply be delivered as part of the Run Phase service. This is a valid argument but even then if we call it service improvement, rather than innovation, it will still need to be carried out *by design* rather than by accident to be successful on a sustainable basis.

Service Life-Cycle Considerations

Service agreements follow a life-cycle approach, which needs to the understood and taken into account when developing an approach to innovation between clients and service providers. A number of industry frameworks describe this (e.g., the Global Sourcing Association's

Outsourcing Life-cycle Model) but few, or any, focus specifically on the context of the delivery of innovation.

For the purposes of this publication, I have used a created a relatively simple life-cycle model, including the following phases:

- **Engagement**—including requirements development, tendering process, supplier selection, contract negotiation, and contract signature activities
- **Transition**—including activities to transfer responsibility of service provision (and potentially people and additional assets if in an outsourcing context) to the service provider
- **Transformation**—including activities to deliver one or more change programs to implement the new supplier's services and/or improve existing improvements to services to achieve the client's business objectives
- **Run**—delivery of ongoing services including continual service improvement and change management activities
- **Renewal/Extension**—activities to implement significant changes to the agreement in terms of scope, timeframe, and/or commercials
- **Exit**—including activities to transfer responsibility of service provision (and potentially people and additional assets if in an outsourcing context) to a different service provider

The phases are also shown in the diagram below.

Service Relationship Life Cycle

As with the whole of the publication, the focus is on how clients and service providers can work together to use innovation to deliver value for both organizations. The client will be looking to derive as much value as it can from the service provider, and the service provider will be looking to achieve higher value for itself by delivering innovative services and innovation that differentiates both itself and the client. The type of value derived from innovation and the actions required to achieve it are likely to be different during the different phases of the life cycle, and so it is important to consider the life-cycle view.

There are opportunities to apply innovation in each of these phases. For example, clients and service providers can use innovative approaches within Transition, Contract Renegotiation, and Exit phases.

For the purposes of this publication, we have focused considerations for innovation and related activities primarily during the Engagement, Transformation, and Run phases of the service relationship life cycle. The later chapter on specific Recommendations has been structured to focus on each of these three phases.

Contractual Considerations

A service agreement is generally based on a legal contract, with set obligations for service provider and client organizations agreed in the Engagement phase of the life cycle.

This often includes a commitment from the service provider to deliver a change program for and/or with the client in the Transformation phase of the life cycle. Depending on the requirements and context, this may include a level of committed innovation.

Once the relationship moves into the Run phase, if not designed appropriately, contractual terms and conditions can create a constraint on ongoing collaborative innovation between clients and service providers.

Equally, the contract can be used to create an enabling framework and incentives for both client and supplier to stimulate the development and delivery of innovation-related activities on an ongoing basis through the Run phase of the life cycle.

Commercial Considerations

Although achieving wider business value through innovation is often an important factor for a client organization when selecting a service provider, the primary client goals for the majority of service agreements focus on achieving a desired quality and level of service, at a specific price point.

Typically, the overall goal is to enable cost savings to be achieved by the client organization, compared to services formerly delivered in-house or by previous service providers.

Similarly, primary service provider goals are likely to be focused on achieving a target level of revenue and profit from the service contract. To achieve target levels of profit, service providers have an incentive to drive cost efficiencies. An additional service provider goal is often to drive profitable revenue growth beyond the base service contract.

Innovation may be required to deliver the change program committed by both parties in the Transformation phase of the service life cycle. The business case for this will typically be built into the commercial agreements underpinning the service contract.

Once in the Run phase of the service life cycle, there is likely to be a commitment from the service provider to deliver a level of ongoing service improvement innovation (noting that not all clients consider service improvement as innovation). For any level of meaningful innovation beyond this, funding and resources will be needed from both parties. This can be particularly challenging for the early stages of joint innovation, such as exploration of challenges and opportunities, idea generation and development, capability prototyping, and viability assessment. These activities will typically be required to demonstrate a sufficiently solid business case to persuade a business sponsor to invest into further development and delivery of the innovation, on the basis of the level of projected benefits.

The commercial pressures on clients and service providers to achieve their primary cost efficiency–related goals from the service relationship can create significant constraints on the willingness and ability of both parties to invest into these early stage joint innovation activities. But without these early stage activities, the business case to invest in follow-on innovation activities to fully develop and deliver innovation will not be clear. If this is the case, it will be challenging to find sponsorship to move forward, and innovation, beyond service improvements and minor incremental change, is likely to be stifled.

In order to overcome these challenges, and achieve innovation beyond the initial Transformation change program, client and service provider organizations will need to collaboratively agree one or more funding mechanisms to support this early stage activity.

My personal view is that both the client and the service provider should provide funding for activities at this stage. This can be achieved through a joint innovation bucket fund or by making decisions on a piecemeal basis. Client organizations may argue the service provider should invest fully in early stage joint innovation, as effectively this is business development–related activity. Service providers may argue the client should invest fully as the focus is on development capability and business case for the client. My argument is that when both parties invest, there will be a higher win rate, as both parties will have skin in the game and care more to ensure they get a solid return on their investments into early stage innovation activities.

One additional commercial pressure in a service relationship can be the consideration of potential competition, once a specific innovation has been jointly developed. Depending on the scope and context, to get best value, clients may wish to open up delivery of change projects and service running of a developed innovation to tender with additional service providers. Service providers considering investing into joint early stage innovation activities will be significantly deterred by such an approach.

Both parties need to carefully consider how they will approach such situations to ensure there is something to be gained from early stage innovation activities for both the client and the service provider organizations. From experience, some items will naturally fit within the domain and strengths of the specific service provider and they will naturally get any follow-on business from the development, delivery, and run. In other cases, it may make more sense for the client to tender for the follow-on activity. The key will be for both organizations to consider how a specific innovation will be managed from the very beginning, *by design*.

Intellectual Property Considerations

Although there are some significant exceptions, the majority of service relationships are non-unique in terms of the scope and type of services provided by a service provider to a client. This provides significant potential for service providers to reuse innovative capabilities developed with one client with their other clients. In this way, innovation, in terms of something new to another client organization (as opposed to new to their industry or new to the world), can often be delivered much more quickly and cost effectively than if totally new capabilities were to be developed.

If the client and service provider do create something new to the world as part of their collaborative innovation activities, it is likely unique intellectual property will be created. It will be important that the partner organizations agree on the approach to be taken for this early in the innovation cycle.

Often, but not always, this will be linked to the source of investment for developing the innovation. For example, if the service provider develops the innovation for the client through its own investment, then frequently the parties will formally agree for the service provider to retain ownership of the intellectual property. Equally, if the innovation has been funded entirely through client investment, typically the parties would agree the client will retain the ownership. Where there is shared investment made, the parties need to carefully agree up front the strategy in regard to the intellectual property developed to avoid falling out and potentially entering into legal disagreements later during the process.

Mutual Knowledge and Insights

One of the key advantages for developing and delivering innovation between client and service provider organizations can be their in-depth knowledge and insight of each other's capabilities, organization, challenges, and opportunities. If both parties are able to harness this knowledge and insight, it can be a hugely powerful enabler for developing innovation with high business value for the client and mutual benefits for the service provider.

At times, this can also be tricky. Both clients and service providers may be able to see the issues and challenges within the other organization, more clearly than the organization can itself. Communicating and receiving such messages can be challenging. The way in which the organizations work together and the relationships between key people across the organizations will be key to success.

In addition, proactivity will be important. Service provider(s) must be proactive and discover what is most important to their clients, and clients need to develop and articulate their business priorities to their service providers and also understand what will motivate their service providers to work with them to deliver innovation over above the core services provided.

CHAPTER 5

Innovation *by Design*

Collaborative Innovation—*by Design*

So far, we've looked at some of the major challenges clients and service providers face when attempting to focus on joint innovation in a service relationship and the specific context and nuances of service relationships. The primary argument of this publication is that when clients and service providers truly collaborate to drive innovation and do this *by design* rather than by accident, they can and do create higher value outcomes for both parties on a repeatable and ongoing basis, throughout the life cycle of their service agreement and relationship.

This chapter describes in detail what we mean by innovation *by design,* as a means for both clients and service providers to work together to deliver successful and sustainable outcomes through managing, developing, and delivering collaborative innovation-related activities.

The approach has been categorized into two parts:

1. Joint innovation governance—focuses on the setup and governance of overall joint innovation–related activities.
2. Joint innovation management and execution—relates to the activities needed to manage, develop, and deliver innovation at a challenge, opportunity, initiative, and/or project level.

The following sections describe and break down each set of activities in detail.

Joint Innovation Governance

This section describes the activities needed to set up and govern the overall approach to joint innovation between the client and service provider *by design.*

Joint innovation governance activities include the following:

- **Agree Approach**—setup of approach and governance—including client and service provider activities to agree innovation definition, scope and initial focus areas in the context of their relationship and how it will be sponsored, funded, developed, delivered, measured, and governed.
- **Manage Governance**—ongoing governance—tracking and supporting progress of current innovation activities, setting of priorities and focus areas for future innovation activities, and measuring the value of and positive communications of delivered innovation activities.

The diagram below highlights the linkage between Joint Innovation Governance and Joint Innovation Management and Execution.

Joint Innovation Management Activities

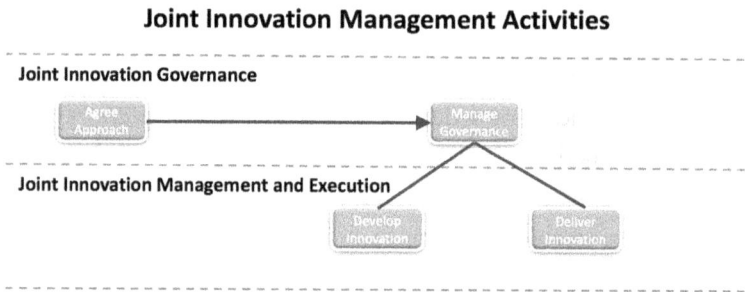

The following subsections describe the recommended Joint innovation governance activities in more detail.

Agree Approach

This section describes the activities a client and a service provider need to undertake to determine and agree how they will jointly manage, develop, and deliver innovation as part of their ongoing relationship. One of the keywords for innovation *by design* is agreement. By consciously agreeing the approach up front, clients and service providers can generate a significant enabler for ensuring sustainable delivery of successful innovation and positive business outcomes throughout the life cycle of their relationship.

Typically, Agree Approach activities will be actioned at the outset of the relationship, during the Engagement phase of the life cycle. However, there is no reason why a client and supplier cannot establish an agreed approach to innovation during the Engagement or Run phases, where an approach had not been previously agreed or where the agreed approach was simply not working, and/or not being adhered to, and needs to be re-established. Similarly, it can be useful to review the approach agreed on a regular basis, for example annually, as part of Manage Governance activities.

Key Agree Approach activities are as follows:

1. Agree Innovation Sponsorship
2. Agree Innovation Definition
3. Agree Initial Scope
4. Agree Initial Innovation Focus Areas
5. Agree Innovation Leadership
6. Agree Innovation Funding Mechanism(s)
7. Agree Manage Governance Approach—including target setting and measurement
8. Agree Joint Innovation Execution Approach

Agree Approach Activities

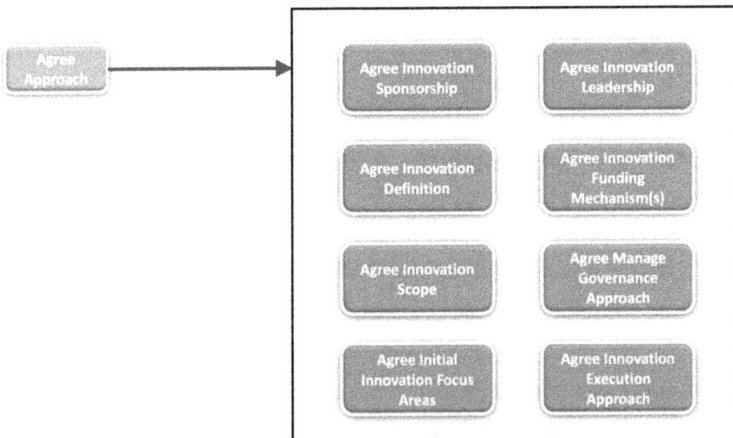

Each set of activities is described in more detail below:

Agree Innovation Sponsorship

"Who will sponsor overall joint innovation activities in the context of the client–service provider relationship?"

Without sponsorship, joint innovation *by design* will not occur. The Innovation Sponsors are typically executive-level personnel in both client and service provider organizations. They should have skin in the game by being in a position to benefit if joint innovation is successfully delivered. Alternatively, they will likely be adversely impacted if it is not.

The sponsors will lead the following steps. The client Innovation Sponsor(s) should develop a definition for joint innovation and verify scope and initial focus areas for joint innovation with the service provider Innovation Sponsor(s), as outlined below, along with agreeing the high-level approach to the leadership, funding, governance, and execution of joint innovation activities.

On an ongoing basis, key inputs from the Innovation Sponsors will include attending regularly scheduled (typically quarterly or half-yearly) executive innovation governance meetings and responding to ad hoc requests from the appointed Innovation Leaders for support and input. The Innovation Sponsors will review progress made, assist with removing any major blockages to progress, measure value and benefits delivered from joint innovation, and set future focus areas for innovation activities, aligned to evolving business priorities.

Agree Innovation Definition

"What does innovation mean in the context of the specific client–service provider relationship?"

As detailed in the Client and Service Provider Challenge chapters, innovation in a client–supplier relationship can be an area fraught with misunderstanding. If a client and a service provider have not actually agreed what innovation means in the context of their relationship, how can the service provider know it is providing it and the client team be confident it is getting it?

By the client and service provider Innovation Sponsors sitting down together and agreeing a simple one-line definition of innovation, in the context of their relationship, with particular emphasis on what innovation means to the client's wider organization, or specific business unit, these misunderstandings can easily be avoided.

There are, of course, many possible definitions, from broad and wide-ranging definitions to ones tied to the very specific goals within the service agreement. A few examples below:

- Innovation is the use of new ideas, or existing ideas in a new context, applied collaboratively by the client and service provider to result in change which delivers business value to the client.
- Innovation is the application of new and emerging technologies developed by the service provider to enable the client's business to increase revenue, reduce cost, and/or improve internal or external customer service ratings.
- Innovation by the service provider for the client will focus on ongoing incremental improvements to the service provider's agreed contracted services for the client, with the objective of either reducing the costs of the service and/or improving agreed levels of service, availability, and/or performance.

A number of client organizations will adopt an existing definition of innovation used by their wider organization. Others will develop a new definition collaboratively with their service provider, Either way, it is important to think this through, write it down, and communicate to teams in both the client and service provider, during the Engagement Phase and very importantly during Transformation and Run Phases of the relationship.

Agree Innovation Scope

"What is the scope for innovation within the context of the client–service provider relationship?"

Once a definition of innovation has been agreed, the next activity is to agree the scope of innovation, in terms of the client's organization. Options can include the following:

- Innovation purely within the scope of the contracted services during the Transformation Phase
- Innovation purely within the scope of the contracted services during the Run Phase delivered as service improvement (noting that some clients will not consider service improvement as innovation)
- Wider innovation within specific business units of the client
- Wider innovation across the entire business organization of the client

Virtually all clients, apart from those in purely simple transactional relationships, will wish to include the first two options listed above. Clients may initially question the third and fourth options and believe the service providers should remain "in their box," that is, focus all innovation-related activity on delivering changes required to deliver the service effectively in the Transformation Phase and on improving the cost efficiency and quality of the service during the Run Phase. This is a valid option and will work for many client relationships.

However, depending on the strengths and capabilities of the service provider, other clients will want more and wish to leverage the relationship they have with the service provider to enable additional value to be delivered to their business unit and/or wider organization, far beyond the scope of contracted services. Obviously, this will also be attractive to the service provider as a potential mechanism for achieving nonorganic growth of its business with the client and may make investment in general and specifically into innovation-related activities with the client, a much more attractive option.

In either case, agreeing the scope for collaborative innovation is an important aspect of innovation *by design*.

Agree Initial Innovation Focus Areas

"In which areas should the client and service provider concentrate innovation-related activity?"

Many studies show that organizations deliver innovation more successfully when they concentrate their efforts in a set number of priority areas, rather than attempt to apply innovation to everything. In line with this, the client should agree with the service provider its preferred initial focus areas for innovation, aligned with its business unit and/or wider organization's business priorities. This is likely to include innovation required to deliver changes needed in the Transformation Phase, and the client and service provider may also set specific initial target focus areas for the Run Phase.

It is likely that the service provider's capabilities will be more aligned with assisting with some of the client's business priorities but not others. When this is the case, it makes sense to limit the agreed focus areas for innovation to ones where the service provider can potentially make a difference and add value. Client organizations with multiple service providers can work across their portfolio of service providers to allocate different focus areas for innovation with each, aligned with their relative strengths and areas of capability.

With the focus areas defined, Joint Innovation Execution activities can more easily be concentrated on identifying specific challenges and opportunities for innovation in the areas that will drive most value for the client and develop ideas, capabilities, and business cases to address them.

One tip from the author here is to include some focus areas where quick wins will be possible. The ability to clearly articulate the value of delivered innovations early in the client–service provider relationship is a great mechanism for gaining wider support and momentum for a joint innovation program.

Agree Innovation Leadership

"Who will be responsible in the client and service provider for making innovation happen in the context of the client–service provider relationship?"

If nobody is made specifically responsible for managing, developing, and ensuring the delivery of joint innovation activities, they are unlikely to happen on a systematic and ongoing basis. As this is the case, it is important to name Innovation Leaders in both the client and service provider.

In large-scale service relationships, the Innovation Leadership roles may be full time. For example, one of my own previous roles in IBM was IBM Innovation Leader for a large financial services organization. In larger relationships, different people may also be made responsible for service improvement and wider scope innovation.

For the majority of service relationships, it is likely the Innovation Leaders in both organizations will also have another wider role to fulfill. This is fine but it is important to ensure the Innovation Leaders, even if part time, in both client and service provider are named and have "managing, developing, and delivering joint innovation" formally set and agreed as part of their overall job role, with priorities set and impact measured as part of their performance appraisals, reviews, and so on. To be effective, the Innovation Leaders need to have a wide skill set (at times they will be facilitators, interpreters, project managers, and so on) and also have excellent networking skills and good network contacts, reputation and knowledge of their own organizations, or the ability to acquire these very quickly.

An excellent way to describe the ideal Innovation Leader is as a T-shaped or TT-shaped professional. The vertical bars in the T and TT represent areas where the professional has a depth of experience in one or more specific technology or business domains or specialisms. The horizontal bar in the T covers the wider skill areas—communication, collaboration, empathy, negotiation skills, and so on. A good Innovation Leader needs both.

One question I have been asked in this area is "Why should the client organization even need to appoint an Innovation Leader?" In response, I'll repeat a point made several times in this publication, as I firmly believe it. Innovation in a collaborative service relationship should not and will not be successfully done to the client. It must be delivered together, with proactive client input and leadership, in addition to proactive input, management, and delivery from the service provider.

Agree Innovation Funding Mechanism(s)

"How will joint innovation activities be funded in the context of the client–service provider relationship?"

Funding for innovation to be delivered during the Transformation Phase will typically be agreed in the core commercial agreement. As this is the case, the primary focus here is for agreeing one or more funding mechanism(s) for activities in the early stages of Joint Innovation Execution during the Run Phase. For example, funding may be needed to review challenges and opportunities, identify and develop ideas, and develop prototype capabilities and business case. This is a stage when sometimes a funding gap develops and it can be a critical one. If there is no or insufficient funding (and resources) to identify and develop potential innovations to demonstrate there is a positive business case for further investment, then joint innovation will flounder.

Once an innovation-related item has been progressed and the business case is proven to be positive, the expectation is that further funding required to develop and deliver the "innovation" would be included in the business case and come from the identified sponsor(s) of the specific initiative (as opposed to the Client and Service Provider Sponsors of overall joint innovation activity described above), as it is the identified sponsor(s) who will reap the benefits of the proposed business case, just as with any other planned program project or change activity.

Potential funding mechanisms for early stage joint innovation activities include an agreed innovation investment "bucket" from the client, service provider, or both, and/or access to wider funds in the client or service provider to develop innovation. For example, IBM has several funded innovation programs that client service account teams can tap into. I've also worked with several clients who have also successfully made use of wider public or industry-based innovation funds to fund working with a service provider to develop new capabilities. There is no harm in having multiple innovation funding mechanisms, as long as the applicability of each is clearly understood. In fact, I'd argue access to multiple funding sources for early stage innovation activity is a positive, as long as the most appropriate source can be agreed and accessed without delaying progress. With innovation, speed of development is often at the heart of the potential business value to be generated.

If the Innovation Leaders are fortunate enough to have an innovation investment "bucket," as my opposite number and I did when I was the IBM Innovation Leader with a financial services client, it is obviously important the money is well spent and results in a number of items reaching the right hand side of the innovation management process funnel that delivers real value. Nobody in the client or service provider will support innovation for innovation's sake, and hopefully the focus on value will be underlined in the agreed joint definition of innovation. It will also be important for the Innovation Leaders to work with the Innovation Sponsors to agree where the available funds are prioritized, that is, in the agreed focus areas or in other areas by exception.

Agree Manage Governance Approach

"How will innovation be reviewed, measured, evolved, and communicated in the context of the client–service provider relationship?"

Ongoing governance will be critical to the success of joint innovation activities. It is important the client and service provider agree the approach to this *by design*, as early as possible in their relationship, if possible during the Engagement Phase. A framework for this may or may not be summarized in specific innovation contract schedules.

Typically, the client and service provider Innovation Leaders, once appointed, will work with the Innovation Sponsors to establish and execute a practical joint innovation governance process during Transformation and Run Phases. To prevent duplication, the majority of content and recommendations for this item is included in the Manage Governance subsection below.

Agree Joint Innovation Execution Approach

"How will innovation be managed, developed, and delivered in the context of the client–service provider relationship?"

The focus here is in agreeing a "process" to systematically progress items from an initial idea, challenge or opportunity through to full implementation, delivery of value, and benefits realization. Direction for this can and should be set in the Engagement Phase. A framework for this may or may not be summarized in specific innovation contract schedules.

Typically, the client and service provider Innovation Leaders, once appointed, will work together to establish and execute a practical joint innovation management and execution process during Transformation and Run Phases. To prevent duplication, the majority of content and recommendations for this item is included in the Joint Innovation Management and Execution subsection.

Manage Governance

This section describes the actions a client and a service provider need to undertake to jointly govern innovation activities, as part of their ongoing relationship.

Key Manage Governance activities are as follows:

1. Executive Innovation Governance
2. Operational Innovation Governance
3. Innovation Target Setting and Measurement
4. Positive Innovation Communications

Manage Governance Activities

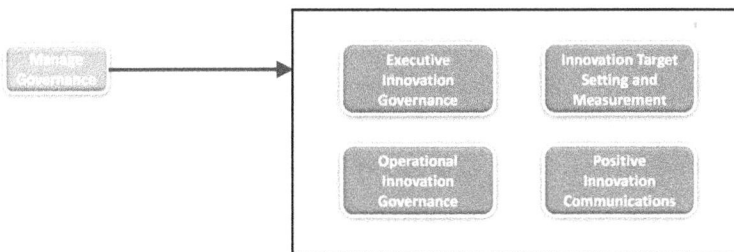

Each set of activities is described in more detail below:

Executive Innovation Governance

"How will the client and service provider oversee innovation activities in the context of the client–service provider relationship?"

Executive governance should be led by the named client and service provider Innovation Leaders, with oversight from the client and service provider Innovation Sponsors. Focus is on reviewing progress, measuring value and benefits realized of existing innovation activities, and setting future focus areas and priorities for innovation.

Executive Innovation Governance meetings typically take place on a quarterly or half-yearly basis, but both the frequency and invitee list for these meetings will vary widely, depending on the context of the client–service provider relationship and agreed scope of joint innovation activities.

Typical Executive Innovation Governance activities include the following:

- Reviewing innovation activity progress
- Addressing major blockers to progress
- Measuring value and benefits realized of delivered innovation activities
- Setting focus areas and priorities for coming period
- Assisting positive communications and celebration of successfully delivered innovation activities

Typically, the Innovation Leaders will lead preparations for the Executive Innovation Governance meetings, including any premeeting stakeholder management activities, if these are required to ensure progress is made during the meetings and successful outcomes from the meetings.

The meeting is intended to be an important part of, and integrated with, overall governance between client and service provider organizations. To be effective, the client and service provider Innovation Sponsors must attend the scheduled Executive Innovation Governance meetings and be empowered with decision-making capability.

If the sponsors are not interested in, or simply cannot prioritize, the meetings to be able to attend, this is probably a clear sign that joint innovation activities are not working and it's time to review whether joint innovation is considered to be a worthwhile priority for both parties. If it is not, then it might be more effective for both parties to focus their limited resources elsewhere. If, as is hopefully the case, joint innovation is considered a priority, particularly by the client organization, then it recommended to revisit the Agree Approach activities described in the previous section.

Outside the window of the Executive Innovation Governance meetings, the Innovation Leaders will typically maintain close communications with the Innovation Sponsors and also make contact with them as needed to help remove blockages to progress, review recommendations to progress innovation outside of agreed focus areas, and assist with other activities as required.

Operational Innovation Governance

"How will the client and service provider proactively drive innovation activities in the context of the client–service provider relationship?"

Operational governance should be managed and owned by the named client and service provider Innovation Leaders. Focus here is on managing Joint Innovation Execution activities from idea, challenge, and opportunity identification and development right through to delivery and benefits realization.

Operational meetings typically take place on a weekly or fortnightly basis but both the frequency and invitee list for these meetings will vary widely, depending on the context of the client–service provider relationship and agreed scope of joint innovation activities.

Typically, standard program and project management tools are used to track items through the innovation management process funnel. A simple spreadsheet can be used for this purpose, with a worksheet for each of the five main Joint Innovation Execution steps, a worksheet for rejected items (detailing the step the item was rejected in and rationale for rejection), and a worksheet for completed items. Items are moved through the worksheets as they progress.

Many visual reporting mechanisms can be used to show current state progress. Examples include many flavors of quadrant chart and mapping of in-progress items to their current step on a visual representation of the Innovation Management Process Funnel. Color-coded keys can be used to highlight alignment to agreed innovation focus areas of in-progress items, alignments with business units, and so on. Simple mobile apps can be created, enabling client and service provider personnel to have real-time access to the latest reports and visuals. The reports will also typically be integrated with wider reporting, portals and mobile apps used by the client and service provider teams.

Innovation Target Setting and Measurement

> *"How will the client and service provider set targets and measure the impact of innovation in the context of the client–service provider relationship?"*

One of the key questions around innovation is "how do we measure it?" As with all measurement systems, there are good ways and there are bad ways. Set the wrong measurements and people can easily focus on the wrong things. In general, the author is not a fan of input-focused measures of innovation. Examples include number of ideas, number of workshops, number of projects, or even percentage of successful projects. These are relatively easy to measure but there is no real measure of the value derived.

The recommendations made here are intended to be pragmatic. It is recommended to measure the value derived from innovation in two ways. One is a hard measure and one a softer one.

The hard measure is to focus measurement on the individual innovation items which progress beyond the Qualify Potential and Business Case step in the joint innovation management process funnel. Each of these must have a business case to move any further forward in the process. The business case will stand on hard measures such as cost savings, increase in revenue, customer retention, specific service key performance indicator measurements, and so on. All of these are clearly measurable and the "innovation" once delivered should be measured for the value delivered and benefits realized, both in absolute terms and against the business case. As these items have been generated and/or significantly accelerated by the focus on joint innovation, a significant element of the benefits realized can quite be rightly attributed to joint innovation activities. Positive results can show the value of joint innovation and any negative results the opposite.

It is noted that this hard measurement sets and measures the objectives and success of individual innovation activities and projects, rather than overall joint innovation activities. However, a small number of very positive returns through delivered innovation activities can soon become a very positive measure of the success of the overall joint focus on innovation.

A softer measure is generally recommended for wider measurement of overall joint innovation between the client and service provider. This can be achieved by use of specific Set-Met objectives and/or formal scores for Client Satisfaction for the client from the service provider, focused on an estimation of the benefits derived from joint innovation activities. It should be noted that such measures do rely on an effective and honest relationship being in place between the client and service provider to work, but such a relationship is also one of the basic prerequisites to ongoing joint innovation *by design*.

There is one point to add on objective setting and measurement of the value of joint innovation. A subset of client and service providers may focus their innovation definition, scope, and focus areas into one specific priority or area. If this is the case, then an overall hard outcome-based objective and measure of success may be easier to define. For example, if innovation is defined as "Use of new ideas to reduce the client's costs" and scope and focus areas of innovation are also specifically targeted onto cost, a cost saving target could be agreed, which would be very measurable. Equally, this would work for revenue generation, customer retention, customer service ratings, and so on. As always, it will depend on the context of the client–service provider relationship.

Positive Innovation Communications

> *"How will successful innovation in the context of the client–service provider relationship be communicated and celebrated?"*

When I worked as a service provider Innovation Leader with a financial services client, the joint innovation work we did was generally very well received by both parties. As a service provider, we consistently achieved an "Exceeded" score for innovation in Set-Met and Client Satisfaction measurements, and the financial services client derived significant business value and benefits realized from a series of joint innovation activities, where both client and service provider teams worked very well together to ensure success.

However, during one Executive Innovation Governance meeting, the client's Innovation Leader and I were politely, but firmly, chastised on one point. The client C-level executive Innovation Sponsor told us both, "You have done a great job in developing innovation and ensuring it is delivered and the value measured but not enough people know about it."

The client, as is often (if not always, please forgive me!) the case, was right. We quickly learned our lesson. After that, each innovation delivered was accompanied by a mini-communications plan to spread the good news and celebrate our joint success. This had a snowball effect. More and more requests came to our joint innovation team to focus on specific client business challenges and opportunities. These had to be filtered, but the positive buzz caused was a good outcome from all concerned.

The message here is simple—positively communicate successful joint innovation. Include in your overall innovation governance approach, and in plans for each innovation which progresses to the right hand side of the funnel, a plan to positively communicate the innovation if it delivers benefits and if appropriate jointly celebrate success.

The author's final tip in this section is to watch out for awards in the client organization, in the service provider organization, and externally, which your joint innovation activities can align to and don't be afraid to enter them. It won't take long for a joint buzz from specific individuals, your teams, and wider businesses winning innovation awards and other awards to be created, and it will be well worth making the effort. And after all, if the joint team has done a great job, why shouldn't they be celebrated and rewarded? More on this later when we discuss the benefits of creating a joint innovation culture.

Joint Innovation Management and Execution

This section describes the actions a client and a service provider need to undertake to determine and agree how they will jointly manage, develop, and deliver individual innovation activities and projects, as part of their ongoing relationship. The key here is for the client and service provider to jointly develop and proactively manage a "process" to systematically progress items from an initial idea, challenge or opportunity through to full implementation, and delivery of value and benefits realization.

Joint Innovation Execution activities include the following:

- **Develop Innovation**—including client and service provider activities to:
  1. Identify ideas, challenges and opportunities for applying innovation
  2. Qualify potential and sponsorship for selected innovation activities
  3. Develop capability and business case for selected innovation activities
- **Deliver Innovation**—including client and service provider activities to:
  1. Implement and deliver selected innovations to enable value to be derived
  2. Realize benefits of innovations delivered

Of course, this is nothing new. It is a practical implementation of the classic Innovation Management Process Funnel, but it is surprising how few clients and service providers adopt such an approach when working together. When implemented effectively and supported by strong sponsorship and governance, as described in the previous section, it is a hugely effective means of developing and delivering joint innovation.

The diagram below maps the key innovation activities outlined earlier to a deliberately simple five-step innovation management process.

Mapping to the Innovation Management Process

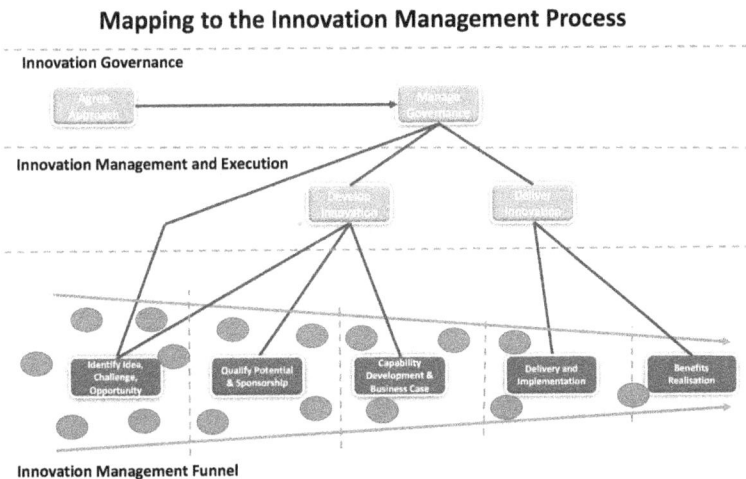

At a summary level, ideas, business challenges, and opportunities for innovation enter the funnel from the left. Typically, these are aligned to the agreed focus areas for joint innovation activity.

Selected items progress through the gated steps of the funnel. Although a relatively large number of items may enter the funnel, the initial steps will be used to identify those with the best sponsorship, business case, expected outcomes, and probability of success. The majority of resource intensive innovation development and delivery activities will then focus on a relatively small number of items, aligned with the client's business priorities. These will be progressed and exit the funnel on the right as delivered innovations, which will then be tracked for their benefits realized.

Equally, the process can be used to fast track selected items through the early stages of development, with the right hand side of the process being an entry point into the client's main program, project, and change management processes.

When reviewing such a joint innovation management process with clients, I've often been asked "Isn't this a process which should run across our organisation and portfolio of service providers and not just with your own service provider organisation?" My answer is always a categorical "yes" to this.

It should be evident that not all innovations within an organization or specific business unit will require collaboration with a specific service provider. The client Innovation Sponsor(s) and Leader(s) are likely to work on a number of innovation initiatives with their different service providers. Sometimes, this will involve working with a single service provider. At other times, the client will be working with multiple service providers on the same innovation initiative. In these circumstances, the client will need to manage innovation effectively across and between its service providers and each service provider be prepared to work with the others for the client's benefit, even if they are sometimes direct competitors with each other.

In these cases, it will be even more important for the clients to drive joint innovation *by design* with their service providers and a structured approach to Joint Innovation Governance and Joint Innovation

Management and Execution will make a huge difference. Personally, I am always very happy when a client organization has a practical innovation management process in place, which crosses service provider boundaries and works. It is much easier to map our specific joint innovation activities onto this, rather than create something new.

When an effective client innovation management process does exist, there will still be benefits of agreeing a practical approach between the client and service provider to integrate with this and verify what will work best in the context of their relationship and the types of innovation it has been jointly agreed should be focused on.

If such an innovation management process does not exist in the client, setting it up with an individual or multiple service provider(s) can also sometimes be a springboard to the wider organization seeing the value of focusing on innovation *by design,* rather than by accident. Of course, for this to happen, the innovations and the business outcomes and benefits delivered need to be well communicated and recognized within the client organization.

In some organizations, I have assisted the wider client organization and/or one or more business unit to subsequently establish their own internal innovation management process, in parallel to setting up a joint innovation management process with my own organization as a service provider.

The following subsections describe the five steps included in the recommended Joint Innovation Management and Execution process funnel required for the development and delivery of innovation between a client and service provider (or multiple service providers).

- **Develop Innovation**—including client and service provider activities to:
  1. Identify ideas, challenges, and opportunities for applying innovation
  2. Qualify potential and sponsorship for selected innovation activities
  3. Develop capability and business case for selected innovation activities

- **Deliver Innovation**—including client and service provider activities to:
    1. Implement and deliver selected innovations to enable value to be derived
    2. Realize benefits of innovations delivered

A key point to stress here is that the Innovation Leaders typically drive, lead, and manage the Develop Innovation activities. In some cases, they may also drive, lead, and manage the Deliver Innovation activities. However, it is more likely these will be carried out by the client and/or service provider's standard program, project, and change management and delivery teams, processes, and capabilities. If this is the case, the role of the Innovation Leaders will include handing over agreed joint innovation activities to the standard program, project, or change teams and then tracking progress during implementation and subsequently ensuring value and benefits realization are tracked, measured, and fed into joint innovation governance.

This is an important distinction to make. As this will be the case for the majority of client–service provider relationships that include a focus on innovation *by design* and is also good practice, this is the assumption made when describing and making recommendations for the Deliver Innovation steps in the following subsections of the document.

Note on the Importance of Design Thinking

"How can we develop and deliver ideas into innovations which will be most valuable for the end users?"

As covered later in this publication, Design Thinking offers a great set of tools, approaches, and resources for developing ideas and delivering innovative capabilities, ensuring they are designed with the end user in mind. More on that later but I thought it useful to flag here as something which should definitely be considered during the Develop and Deliver innovation steps.

Identify Idea, Challenge, or Opportunity

This section describes the Develop Innovation actions a client and a service provider need to undertake to identify ideas, challenges, and opportunities to develop them into innovation-related activities.

Funding for this step will generally come from a joint investment in time and people from the client and service provider. The general intention is to progress through the step quickly, with the minimum of investment.

The truth of the matter is there should be no shortage of ideas. This activity is all about identifying the best sources of ideas, identifying existing ideas, and generating new ones. It will be important, in most cases, to align idea generation with the priority challenges and opportunities of the client's business, as identified in the activities described in the previous section to agree focus areas for innovation.

Do not be afraid of the odd exception, which comes in from left field and does not align with the agreed focus areas but everyone feels has great potential business value. Ideas such as this should always be considered and, if necessary, taken to the Innovation Sponsors to agree as an exception to follow up. I'm a great believer in relying on the faith and judgment of the Innovation Leaders on the ground to know which bets to follow and which to leave well alone.

Key activities in this area include the following:

- Identifying Idea Sources
- Idea Generation
- Idea Assessment

Identify Idea, Challenge, Opportunity Activities

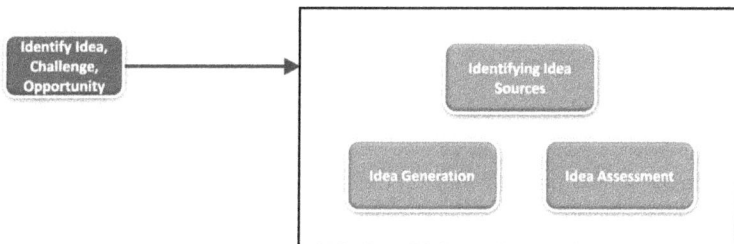

Identifying Idea Sources

"Where do the best ideas come from in the context of the client–service provider relationship?"

The answer to this question is probably that good ideas can come from many different places. The best sources will vary depending on the context of the client and service provider, scope of the service, and so on. The following list highlights many potential sources of ideas. Apart from the first item, the applicability and the ordering will depend on the context of the specific service and relationship.

- The client's business challenges and opportunities—OK, these aren't ideas themselves yet, but they are the best source for generating them
- The client's employees in the business unit(s) to whom the service is delivered to
- The client's employees in the wider organization
- The service provider's employees in the account team for the client
- The service provider's employees supporting other clients
- The service provider's employees in the wider organization
- The client's customers
- Organizations in the same industry as the client—what is the client's competition doing differently?
- Organizations providing similar services as the service provider—what is the service provider's competition doing differently?
- Organizations in different industries to the client—what can be learned and reused from other industries?
- Third-party organizations—consultants, specialist organizations, and so on
- Research organizations and academia
- The general public
- And so on . . .

There is also the possibility (and I don't usually use the phrase but it works here) of thinking outside the box, when considering sources of ideas. Forgive me now for this little aside but I think it is a useful one. I would describe one additional great source of ideas I've had personal experience of using as "unconstrained bright young people." Specifically, I've had the pleasure and privilege of being the lead mentor for a series of IBM Extreme Blue innovation projects.

IBM Extreme Blue assigns mixed business and technology teams of top talent student interns to work on an internal IBM or client challenge or opportunity. I've used the program to benefit a number of client organizations. The teams are mixed with both business- and technology-focused interns. They are tasked with developing ideas around a specific client challenge and subsequently to select one specific targeted idea to focus on. The team then works with the client, supported by IBM mentors and experts, to create a working prototype in a matter of weeks, along with a supporting business case white paper.

The interns lack the detailed business and technology understanding of the combined client and IBM team but are blissfully inhibited by the constraints and baggage we all begin to carry, without even noticing it over the years. To them, anything is possible. Time after time, I have seen this approach develop ideas and working capabilities which would simply not have been created without the application of such bright unconstrained minds. If you can tap into an existing program such as IBM Extreme Blue, I would recommend it. It's a great experience. If not, you could consider how to replicate such an approach, for example, using your own apprentices, interns or graduate trainees, and so on. Aside complete.

As outlined above, the best sources of ideas will vary between service relationships. It will be important for the client and service provider Innovation Leaders to regularly review the overall list of sources of ideas, add unlisted relevant sources, and create a short list of the best sources for ideas in the context of their own specific client–service provider relationship. Once this is done, the next step will be to determine how best to practically tap into each source to generate ideas, aligned to jointly agreed focus areas for innovation.

Idea Generation

"How can we generate ideas in the context of the client–service provider relationship?"

Once a solid set of sources for good ideas has been identified, the obvious next step is to begin using them to generate ideas for innovation. One of the most effective approaches will be to focus use of the idea sources to generate ideas against a set of challenges and opportunity areas. The good news is that by already agreeing a set of focus areas for joint innovation, aligned with the client's business priorities and the service provider's strengths, the joint team already have a great place to start.

If the focus areas can be broken down, with input from the Innovation Sponsors and others into relatively specific challenges and/or opportunities, this will be even better, as it will give a very clear direction for idea generation activities.

There are many ways to generate ideas. For example:

- Talking to people in the key idea source groups—such an obvious suggestion but not always done; this could include one to one interviews, speaking to people as they do fulfill their role, employee shadowing, and so on
- Requesting ideas and inputs—for example, using paper, online, and app-based idea boxes, questionnaires, and surveys
- Face-to-face idea generation workshops—potentially using a variety of ideation, creativity, and/or Design Thinking techniques
- Online idea generation systems and events—these can vary greatly from fully secure closed events with selected invitees to full-on open innovation crowd-sourcing events, and all points between
- And so on . . .

This publication would be too long if it attempted to detail and describe many of the possible approaches. Instead, a real-life example is included below. This builds across all five steps of the recommended Joint Innovation Management and Execution process.

Whichever idea generation approaches are used, three simple steps should be followed:

1. Prepare well—typical activities include understanding the focus area, having the right core of people included, plus additional subject matter experts, sponsors, and other groups as and when required, and communicating clearly with attendees beforehand to set expectations.

2. Execute professionally—facilitate idea generation activities effectively, keep people engaged whatever medium used, provide subject matter expert inputs and feedback as and when required, tease out further details, and encourage collaboration to develop ideas further.

3. Follow up quickly—the best idea generation efforts, whatever the medium, will be spoiled and credibility lost for the future if follow up is not fast and effective or prioritized actions are not well communicated to those who participated.

Idea Assessment

"How can we assess ideas to ensure we follow up on the right ones?"

Over the years, I've seen some quite complex idea-scoring mechanisms. Generally, I'm not a huge fan of using them. As always, it's the value, or early on in the process the potential value which counts. More often than not, experienced people, such as the Innovation Leaders in the client and service provider organization, can make better judgments on the potential value than scoring mechanisms, however well-constructed.

My experience of being a service provider Innovation Leader with a financial services client taught me the value of using a pragmatic approach. Intuition matters. If my opposite number and I both considered an idea had solid potential value, aligned with our jointly agreed focus areas for innovation and would likely be achievable, we backed it. We would do this, even if in our own scoring mechanism, the item may have scored lesser than another idea, which we didn't have such a good feel for. Of course, this could have been an argument for improving our scoring system but hopefully you get the point.

Having said that, scoring mechanisms can be useful. For example, a scoring mechanism can be used as a fast filter when the team is inundated with ideas and does not have the time or resources to review them all. In this case such an approach can help by enabling the joint team to focus their effort on reviewing a smaller number of ideas, spending more time assessing the viability of each one than would have otherwise been possible.

Practical Real-World Example

This example is based on innovation activity within a real-life client–service relationship. As with the other real-life examples in the Proof Points chapter, details of the client and service provider have been anonymized. The example begins here and then continues through the five sections covering Joint Innovation Management and Execution.

A large retail organization had a service agreement with an IT service provider to deliver and support a range of IT services for its retail store and head office–based business units. Several years into this relationship, the client and service provider agreed they should increase focus on joint innovation activities. As the client had a relatively large number of physical stores, the two organizations agreed to make the store a focus area for innovation activity.

Both organizations appointed a lead for this activity, referred to below as the client and service provider Innovation Leaders. The Innovation Leaders recognized the store a wide focus area for potential innovation. They worked with the client's retail and IT business units to identify specific challenges or opportunities that would be good targets for innovation activity. As improving customer service was a key priority for the client's business, the joint team agreed to use this to form the basis of a joint innovation challenge, creating the following working question: "How can technology be used to improve and deliver great customer service in the store?" This gave the joint team a very clear steer where joint innovation should focus, with the added advantage of not constraining the ideas that could be developed to address the challenge.

The Innovation Leaders reviewed a number of potential idea sources and developed a prioritized list. This included the client's customers, the client's employees in the stores, client and service provider support staff, and a number of secondary sources, such as the activities of competing organizations.

For each idea source, the Innovation Leaders developed an approach for idea generation. For the purposes of this publication, we'll focus on the client's employees in the stores as an example source of ideas. These were frequently surveyed for feedback, and so the survey results were reviewed to determine potential ideas that could be generated from existing data.

To gain greater insight, the Innovation Leaders also spent time in a number of stores, shadowing and talking in detail to employees about their challenges and discussing with the employees their experiences of using existing technologies deployed in the store and their ideas for changes and new capabilities to enhance customer service. One of the outputs of this activity was also a long list of identified challenges, which answered a slightly different question from the one which the team started with. This could be summarized as, "How is technology preventing great customer service in the store?"

Subsequently, the Innovation Leaders planned and ran a series of face-to-face innovation workshops with client employees from across many stores. Further workshops were also run with support staff and retail subject matter experts. A number of techniques were applied during the facilitated workshops, such as the Lotus Blossom method of beginning with a central challenge and working out from the middle (of the flower) to identify more specific challenges and collaboratively generating ideas to address.

The output of the above activity was a set of prioritized challenges and identification of a large number of ideas of how they could be overcome, along with additional totally new ideas not linked with current business processes and activities. The ideas were focused on addressing—"How can technology be used to improve and deliver great customer service in the store?"

Follow-on activity included assessing the ideas, selecting a list of prioritized ideas, and communicating the results to the teams who had taken part and input into the process.

Progression to Next Step

"We've identified an idea which we think has real potential, what do we do now?"

The output of the step described above should be one or more prioritized ideas, ready for the value to be further qualified, and one or more potential sponsors identified.

Proceed to the next step of the innovation management funnel process. Read on . . .

Qualify Potential and Sponsorship

This section describes the Develop Innovation actions a client and a service provider need to undertake to qualify the potential and sponsorship for an idea.

The input into this step should be one or more prioritized ideas, ready for the value to be further qualified, and one or more potential sponsors identified.

Funding for this step will generally come from a joint investment in time and people from the client and service provider. The general intention is to progress through this step quickly, with the minimum amount of effort and cost the team can get away with.

So, now we have an idea. What do we practically do with it? This is really where the hard work starts.

Key activities in this area include the following:

- Qualify Potential
- Verify Sponsorship and Support

Qualify Potential and Sponsorship Activities

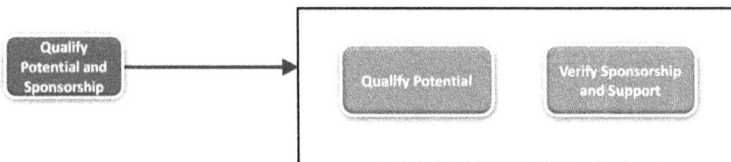

These activities will be carried out in parallel on an iterative basis, rather than as separate linear steps.

Qualify Potential

"How can we verify ideas to ensure we follow up on the right ones?"

In the previous section, we highlighted the potential use of scoring mechanisms; but in this Qualify Potential and Sponsorship step, the activities are more about knuckling down, developing, and reviewing the idea in more detail. Typically, this involves engaging domain and wider subject matter experts to consider the idea and generally pull it apart to see if it really stands up to scrutiny.

The activity here includes a number of detailed activities:

- First, doing whatever is needed, without expending "too much" money and effort, to understand what will be needed to develop and deliver the idea.
- Second, verifying how achievable is this and in what sort of time frame it could be delivered.
- Third, the team needs to verify how real the potential value and benefits may be.
- It's important not to be too positive or negative about the idea during these activities. Objectivity can be hard to achieve but will pay dividends later. If needed, take a step back and/or get a second or even a third opinion. The likelihood is when a batch of ideas are put through this level of scrutiny, only a percentage of them will survive.

Verify Sponsorship and Support

"How can we assess ideas to ensure we follow up on the right ones?"

For ideas that look like they may be viable, there are still hurdles to overcome before putting significant investment into them. Probably, the most important action is the verification of *potential* sponsorship. At this stage, the team may have a high level of idea of the costs and benefits involved but not the level of detail a potential sponsor would need to be to consider any significant investment. But there is little point in funding further capability and business case development until one or more sponsors confirm that if the capability, once developed, works and the business case flies, they will be willing to invest part of their hard-won budget to turn the idea into a reality and later reap the benefits.

The activity here is all about developing and showcasing the idea, along with the associated high-level potential business case to one or more potential sponsor(s) in the client. What is the minimum the sponsor would need to see to get really interested?

Technology advances in recent years have really helped here. Depending on the specific innovation, cloud computing, app platforms, and fast app prototyping can be used in combination to show something which looks real, without any major or ongoing investment.

It will pay to demonstrate to the potential sponsor(s) the team has done its homework and has the support of people the sponsor(s) trust. These are the people who know what works and what doesn't in their business. It is likely you may have already worked with some of them when qualifying potential. If so, work with them to confirm their support. If not, engage them now and get their input.

If the potential sponsors do put their thumbs up, great, move onto the next step. Better still, look to persuade them to, if possible, part-invest in the next stage of development of the capability and business case. One important lesson I've learned is when people have a stake in the game and have spent some of their own budget, they tend to be much more interested in and supportive of what happens afterward.

If the potential sponsor(s) don't support or are only lukewarm, my advice is to park the idea and move onto some of the others ones on the list. Significant investment should not have been made by this stage, as the next step is where the real spending usually starts. Cut your losses and don't feel bad. It's better to fail fast, than fail very publicly and slowly later on in the process.

One other point to make here. The onus above is focused on finding sponsorship in the client. It's also important to ensure support within the service provider organization. It would not be a great experience for anyone if a client sponsor became very excited but then the wider service provider organization, for whatever reason, doesn't want to take the idea further. So, ensure the service provider Innovation Sponsor is equally supportive. If there is a significant potential sale or increase in revenue for the service provider from the idea once delivered, you may also be able to persuade them to coinvest further into the innovation development too.

Practical Real-World Example

This is a continuation of the example described in the previous step.

The Innovation Leaders reviewed the viability of the shortlist of prioritized challenges and ideas to "improve and deliver great customer service in the store" with a series of client and service provider retail business and technology experts. A little initial work was carried out to verify what would be needed to be done to develop, prove, and implement the ideas and verify likely timescales.

On the basis of this analysis, some ideas were discounted. The remaining selected ideas were categorized between quick wins and items that would need more significant investment and time to develop and deliver.

In parallel, the impact of the challenges and the benefits of implementing the ideas were reviewed. In some cases, it was possible to begin development of a hard business case. In other cases, benefits were harder to quantify in numerical terms but could be articulated in other ways.

Support was confirmed in the service provider organization for further developing a set of the selected ideas. A small number of these ideas were categorized as service improvement activities, which the service provider took the responsibility for development and delivery of, working with the client team. A number of the other ideas, if taken forward by the client, would potentially result in business growth opportunities for the service provider.

The selected ideas were packaged into a communications pack. The remaining ideas were categorized between quick-win innovations and longer term innovation opportunities, with a high-level outline business case shown for each. The Innovation Leaders presented these to potential sponsor(s) in the client organization.

Feedback was very positive. It was agreed that the longer term innovation opportunities would be fed directly into strategic planning (effectively moving them into the Develop Capability and Business Case step with an aim for longer term delivery). The sponsor(s) recognized the benefit of the quick-win innovations, but there was a problem. Budget allocation had already been made for the year and this client–service provider relationship did not have a "bucket" for innovation activity. The client sponsor(s) took a decision to reallocate an element of its budget to develop the capability and business case for the quick-win innovations to verify their potential (effectively moving them into the Develop Capability and Business Case step with an aim for fast delivery).

Progression to Next Step

"We've qualified the potential value and sponsorship for an idea, what do we do now?"

The output of this step should be one or more qualified ideas, with one or more potential sponsor(s) in the client organization confirmed and support in the service provider organization confirmed.

Proceed to the next step of the innovation management funnel process. Read on . . .

Develop Capability and Business Case

This section describes the Develop Innovation actions a client and a service provider need to undertake to develop a capability and business case for a qualified idea, up to a level where the identified potential sponsor(s) will be willing to fund any further development activity needed plus implementation and delivery actions, based on the positive business case created.

The input into this step should be one or more qualified ideas, with one or more potential sponsor(s) in the client organization identified and agreed and support in the service provider organization confirmed.

Funding for this step can come from multiple sources. If a "bucket" fund exists for innovation activities, this step is where the majority of this budget will be allocated. Some clients and service providers, such as IBM, also have wider innovation programs, which can be tapped into to gain funding for innovation development activities.

One excellent source of funding is investment from potential sponsor(s), convinced by activities in the previous steps that the idea is worth investing in because of the likely potential benefits. Such an investment will give the sponsor(s) a real motivation to move forward if the capability and business case development activities from this step deliver positive results.

While, typically, the previous two steps can be progressed quickly without investing significant resources or money, this step will likely take a level of time, effort, and hard cash.

Key activities in this area include the following:

- Develop and Prove Capability
- Hone Business Case

Develop Capability and Business Case Activities

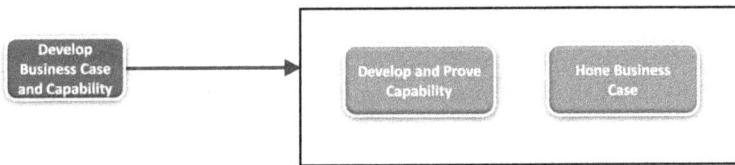

These activities will be carried out in parallel on an iterative basis, rather than as separate linear steps.

There may be questions here about potential overlap with the activities in the previous step. This is a good point. The guidance provided in this book is to create a gated joint innovation management process funnel but this will need to be tailored for each client–service provider relationship. The points where one step begins or ends in different organizations may be at different points, depending on the context and views of the client and service provider. One size doesn't fit all. The team will need to work out what works best in its own relationship and context.

In addition, often innovation management is an iterative process and items may move back a step at times as well as forward. The recommendation is to be pragmatic. Use this publication as guidance, alongside inside knowledge of what will work and what won't in the context of the specific client–service provider relationship.

Develop and Prove Capability

"How do we develop the idea to prove capability?"

The answer to this question is really "how long is a piece of string?" or the classic "it depends." The activity here may include development work to get the capability working in a test environment, activity to create a prototype capability, activity to create a proof of concept capability, or even get to the stage of running a live pilot. What is needed will depend on the size, shape, and scope of the specific innovation being developed and on the program, project, and change management processes in the client and service provider organizations.

The objective of the activity is to prove, and often fast track, the capability to a sufficient level that the business case can be further qualified and the innovation developed can be handed over to "standard" program, project, and change management activities to further develop and test before implementing into the "live" or "production" environment.

As outlined in the previous step, technology advances in recent years can help greatly here. Depending on the specific innovation, cloud computing, app platforms, and fast app prototyping can be used in combination to show something which looks real, without major or ongoing investment.

Hone Business Case

"How do we develop the business case?"

Creation of business cases is such a common activity; there is little benefit in detailing "how to" recommendations here. Developing a business case for a new innovation should be little different from developing business cases for other change activity, although risk and contingency elements may need to be adjusted, particularly if it is a new to the world capability, rather than a new to the client capability which the service provider has already successfully implemented in partnership with other clients.

In terms of a specific client–service provider relationship, there can sometimes be a question of trust. How much information should the client share with the service provider? Commercial sensitives will always exist and need to be sensibly thought through and managed; but if the trust can be developed, there can be significant benefits to both parties from a level of transparency.

These things are always best practically highlighted through use of real-world examples. Here is an example focused on concerns over sharing information during business case development.

A service provider developed a new to the world innovation capability which it believed would be ideal for a "first of a kind" style deployment in a client's environment. The Innovation Leader of the service provider approached a potential client sponsor and suggested they jointly develop a business case. The client sponsor politely responded by saying he or she was simply not willing to share cost profiles, which were key to the business case, with the service provider. The service provider was also a little reticent to share certain information from its side, due to the newness of the capability and concerns over intellectual capital.

As the two worked together and trust grew, the service provider Innovation Leader developed an assumed business case, estimating likely cost items and numbers on the client side and including early pricing details from the service provider side and shared this with the client sponsor. The client sponsor reviewed the business case and highlighted line items that the sponsor considered were too low or too high and added in a couple of missed items. Seeing the numbers actually looked very positive, the client sponsor quickly agreed to fund further implementation and delivery work on the back of the business case.

Practical Real-World Example

This is a continuation of the example described in the previous steps.

The client sponsor(s) took the decision to reallocate a small element of budget to develop the capability and business case for the identified quick-win innovations to verify potential.

The client and service provider teams worked together to develop and test a number of capabilities that came from the initial challenges and ideas. Some of these could be considered as incremental changes, others as new to the client innovations, and some as new to the world innovations. The capabilities were tested and introduced into the client's store testing environments. In parallel, the client and service provider teams worked to harden the business case in line with the results from testing.

The capabilities for the majority of the selected quick-win ideas were proven and the associated business case agreed. The client sponsors made a decision to reallocate a further amount of budget to implement and deliver the quick-win innovations into the live environment across the store estate.

Progression to Next Step

"We've developed the capability and proven the business case, what do we do now?"

The output of this step should be one or more "innovations" ready for implementation, that is, developed and proven capability (new to the client and/or new to the world) with a hardened business case for one or more qualified ideas, with agreement from sponsor(s) in the client organization to fund implementation and delivery.

Proceed to the next step of the innovation management funnel process. Read on . . .

Implement and Deliver

This section describes the Deliver Innovation actions a client and a service provider need to undertake to implement and deliver an "innovation" developed from an idea progressed through the previous Develop Innovation steps of the innovation management process funnel.

The input into this step should be one or more "innovations" ready for implementation, that is, developed and proven capability (new to the client and/or new to the world) with a hardened business case for one or more qualified ideas, with agreement from sponsor(s) in the client organization to fund implementation and delivery.

Typically, this is where the client and service provider Innovation Leaders hand over their work to "standard" program, project, and change management teams, capabilities, and processes in the client and/or service provider organizations, as the "innovation" will need to be implemented in the same way as any other change.

The implementation activity may include any further development and testing required and change and delivery activities to introduce the "innovation" into the live environment, plus any changes required to service, support, and operational teams, capabilities, and processes to enable the "innovation" to be supported, once live.

Funding for this step typically comes from the agreed client sponsor(s) of the "innovation," as detailed in the business case. This may or may not result in sales and/or revenue growth for the service provider organization, depending on the specific "innovations" and fit with the existing commercial agreement between the client and service provider.

The client and service provider Innovation Leaders keep a watching brief on this activity, working in partnership with program, project, and change teams.

Practical Real-World Example

This is a continuation of the example described in the previous steps.

The Innovation Leaders handed over the quick-win "innovations" developed and tested in the previous step to the store change management and improvement program. The "innovations" were further tested, and operational support procedures agreed and developed. The "innovations" were then integrated into the standard storewide release program of capability changes and upgrades and over a series of weeks implemented across the large portfolio of stores.

The outcome of this activity was that the quick-win "innovations" were successfully implemented and a range of benefits delivered in the stores, which "improved and delivered great customer service in the store."

The longer term "innovations" continued to be progressed as part of longer term strategic change plans for the store environment, with a number of them implemented in the following periods.

Progression to Next Step

"We've implemented the capability, what do we do now?"

The output of this step should be one or more "innovations" implemented and delivered in the live environment, delivering value and benefits to the client organization (and potentially sales and revenue to the service provider).

Proceed to the next step of the innovation management funnel process. Read on . . .

Realize Benefits

This section describes the Deliver Innovation actions a client and a service provider need to undertake to measure the benefits realized from an "innovation" developed from an idea progressed through the previous Develop and Deliver Innovation steps of the innovation management process funnel.

The input into this step should be one or more "innovations" implemented and delivered in the live environment, delivering value and benefits to the client organization.

Typically, the client and service provider Innovation Leaders will work with standard program, project, and change management teams, capabilities, and processes in the client and/or service provider organizations, to measure, quantify, and assess the benefits derived from the "innovation" in the same way as any other change.

The client and service provider Innovation Leaders feed the output of this activity into reporting and Executive Innovation Governance activities. It will be important to investigate further any innovations not delivering to their business cases and take remedial action if or as required. The benefits and value of innovations delivered will be a key element of measurement in governance.

The benefits of successfully delivered innovations should also be positively communicated, and success should be celebrated as part of innovation governance.

Practical Real-World Example Copy

This is a continuation of the example described in the previous steps.

The Innovation Leaders worked with client business and client and service provider service teams to verify the impact of the "innovations" delivered to ensure benefits were being realized and the business case met.

The outcome of this activity was fed into reporting and governance, and the outcomes were positively communicated within client and service provider organizations. The outcomes were used as input into increased scores for innovation in Client Satisfaction and Set-Met governance mechanisms. The positive outcome of the innovation activity was communicated within the client and service provider organizations, and the project was nominated for an award within the client organization.

Life-Cycle Mapping

As described in the previous chapter, the service life cycle is a key characteristic of client–service provider relationships. Innovation activities can be aligned with the life-cycle phases previously described as outlined below. The primary focus for innovation-related activity is within the Engagement, Transformation, and Run phases.

Innovation Activities During Engagement Phase

Focus in the Engagement phase includes the following:

- **Agree Approach**—including client and service provider activities to define what innovation means in the context of their relationship, the scope and priorities for joint innovation activities, and how it will be sponsored, funded, developed, delivered, measured, and governed during Transformation and Run phases. This may include agreement on specific innovation contract schedules.
- **Develop Innovation**—including activities required to enable innovation to be developed and delivered, particularly during the Transformation phase. Activities here are likely to be limited because at this stage the service provider has no commitment, sponsorship, or funding from the client.

The diagram below shows recommended innovation-related activities during the Engagement phase.

Innovation Activities During Engagement Phase

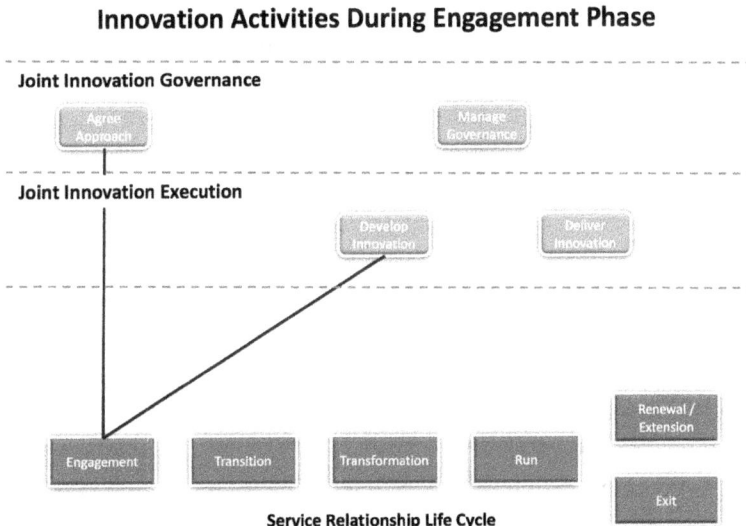

Joint Innovation Governance

Agree Approach   Manage Governance

Joint Innovation Execution

Develop Innovation   Deliver Innovation

Renewal / Extension

Engagement   Transition   Transformation   Run

Exit

Service Relationship Life Cycle

Innovation Activities During Transformation Phase

Focus in the Transformation phase includes the following:

- **Develop Innovation**—including client and service provider activities to develop and prove solutions and capabilities (or reuse existing supplier capabilities in client context) to be delivered during initial Transformation program. The focus areas for innovation to be delivered during the Transformation phase and many of the specific solutions and capabilities to be deployed will most likely have been preagreed during the Engagement phase. In certain circumstances, significant activity to develop new capability may be required, particularly when the Transformation phase includes development and delivery of first kind of capabilities.
- **Deliver Innovation**—including change activities required to deliver the innovation to enable the benefits to be realized during the Transformation phase.
- **Manage Governance**—including governance of innovation-related activities during the Transformation phase. This should be closely integrated with overall governance and includes tracking and measurement of the value of innovation-related activity and positive communications of the innovations delivered during the Transformation phase.

The diagram below shows recommended innovation-related activities during the Transformation phase.

Innovation Activities During Transformation Phase

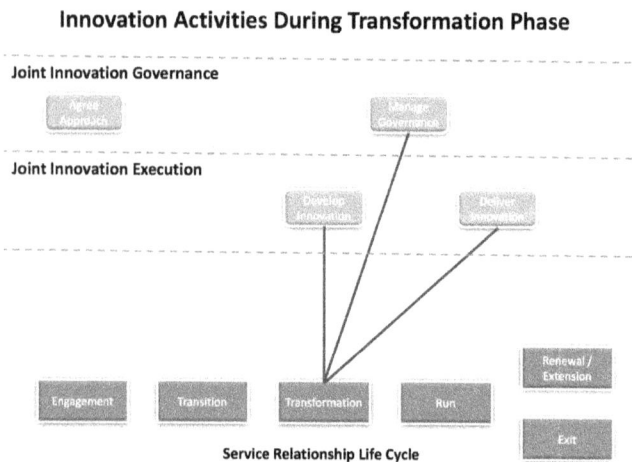

Joint Innovation Governance

Agree Approach   Manage Governance

Joint Innovation Execution

Develop Innovation   Deliver Innovation

Engagement   Transition   Transformation   Run   Renewal / Extension   Exit

Service Relationship Life Cycle

Innovation Activities During Run Phase

Focus in the Run phase includes the following:

- **Develop Innovation**—including client and supplier activities to identify ideas, challenges, and opportunities to apply innovation, develop and prove solutions and capabilities (or reuse existing supplier capabilities in client context), and develop business case for delivery.
- **Deliver Innovation**—including change activities required to deliver the innovation to enable the benefits to be realized during the Transformation phase.
- **Manage Governance**—including ongoing governance of innovation-related activities during the Run phase. This should be closely integrated with overall governance and includes tracking and measurement of the value of innovation-related activity and positive communications of the innovations delivered during the Run phase.

The diagram below shows recommended innovation-related activities during the Run phase.

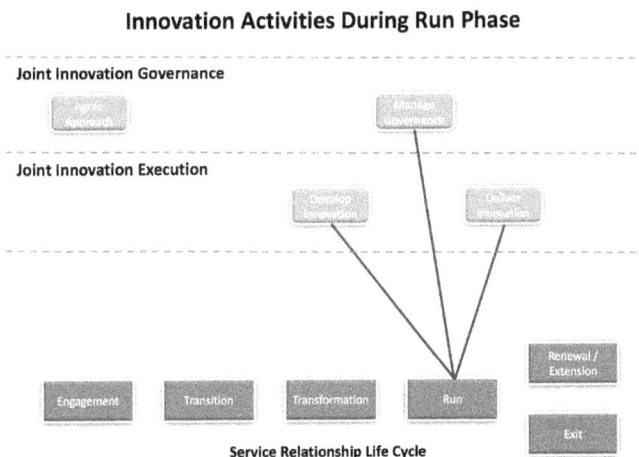

Innovation Activities During Run Phase

Innovation Activities During Transition, Renewal/Extension, and Exit Phases

Primary innovation activities in these phases of the client–service provider relationship life cycle have not been mapped out specifically.

- **Transition Phase**—there may be significant innovation-related activity during the Transition Phase; this will follow the same pattern as described above for the Transition Phase.
- **Renewal/Extension**—to some extent the Renewal/Extension Phase is a repeat of the Engagement Phase, although client and service provider will have much greater knowledge of each other than in a totally new engagement. Renewal/Extension negotiations may include the development of a new Transformation program and the development of changes to the current Run approach to innovation. The innovation-related activity during the Renewal/ Extension will, therefore, follow the same pattern as described above for the Engagement Phase.
- **Exit Phase**—can there really be innovation within the Exit Phase? The client will certainly be motivated but the service provider less so. However, I have witnessed a number of excellent innovation-related projects and activities successfully delivered as part of exit activity, particularly where transfer of services to another service provider has a level of complexity. A key consideration for the client is likely to be ensuring there is sufficient motivation for the service provider they are exiting from to make the exit succeed.

CHAPTER 6

Proof Points

Introduction

The previous chapter described a structured approach for achieving innovation *by design* as part of a collaborative relationship between a client and service provider, including use of a real-life example that spanned across the suggested steps for Joint Innovation Management and Execution. This chapter provides further examples and proof points of joint innovation activities between clients and service providers. All are based on real examples, although the identities of the clients and service providers have been anonymized.

Negative examples can sometimes be as powerful, if not more so, than positive ones. Chapters Two and Three highlighted the fact that there are a number of challenges that face clients and service providers attempting to focus on collaborative innovation. To reflect these points, we begin this chapter with an example of failed joint innovation activities, in the belief the lessons learned from this will be very useful when considering how to, and how not to, approach innovation *by design*.

The subsequent examples are positive ones, with one highlighting a successful wide-ranging joint innovation program and one showcasing a specific successful joint innovation project.

Failed Joint Innovation Activity

I considered it important to include at least one strong "how not to" example in this publication. There are many potential pitfalls we could highlight but which should we focus on? There is also a need to respect client and service provider sensitivities and protect their identities. Taking these factors into account, I've opted for the approach of creating a blended example, which takes input from several real-life relationships, involving a range of different clients and service providers.

Engagement Phase

Following a highly competitive Engagement Phase, a client in a financial services industry and a service provider agreed a long-term services agreement. There was much discussion on "innovation" during the Engagement Phase, and a contract schedule was created.

- This described how both parties would appoint named Sponsors and Leaders for innovation and agree a detailed approach to joint governance during the Transformation Phase to prepare for an ongoing focus on joint innovation during the Run Phase.
- Agreed Transformation Phase change program and Run Phase service improvement activities were specifically excluded from innovation-related activities.
- The agreement did not detail how funding for innovation would be obtained.

Transition and Transformation Phase

The two parties worked together through Transition and Transformation Phases. Both the client and service provider nominated Innovation Sponsors. An initial Innovation Executive Governance meeting was scheduled three months after the commencement of the Transformation change program. This meeting was well attended by the named Innovation Sponsors and by many client and service provider managers and team representatives. At this stage, neither client nor service provider had named an Innovation Leader.

The meeting was scheduled to run for one hour. The first 45 minutes were dominated by a long discussion on current challenges in the Transformation program, although this was outside the scope of the Innovation Executive Governance meeting agenda. The attendees agreed the final 15 minutes should focus on what the meeting was billed to be about—how both parties would work together to initiate joint innovation activities. A member of the service provider team asked the client team what was most important to their business, suggesting this should be where both parties focus joint innovation activity. Members of the client team responded by suggesting the service provider team should be telling them where innovation should be focused, taking input from their knowledge of the client's business developed in the Transition Phase and early stages of the Transformation Phase change program and from the experience of working with similar clients. The meeting ran out of time. No firm actions were agreed.

Three months passed. There were less attendees at the second Innovation Executive Governance meeting, as those not needing to be there were sensibly dropped from the invitee list. The key Innovation Sponsors from the client and service provider did attend. There was a short conversation at the beginning of the meeting when the client team raised frustrations with elements of the service provider's performance in the Transformation program. The attendees then focused on the set agenda of the meeting. The major item on the agenda was how both parties would work together to initiate joint innovation activities. Since the last meeting, the service provider had nominated a part-time Innovation Leader, with the innovation responsibilities being fitted in alongside his or her role in the Transformation change program, but the client had not named an Innovation Leader.

In response to the client's challenge in the previous meeting, the service provider had developed and, during the meeting, presented a set of recommendations for four initial potential focus areas for joint innovation following the Transformation change program. The client discounted two of these areas and added one other. All agreed this was a positive discussion. The joint team now had three agreed focus areas for innovation activities.

The service provider Innovation Leader asked the client Sponsors who they should work with in the client organization to identify specific challenges and opportunities in the agreed focus areas, as this would enable the joint team to identify and develop an initial set of ideas, including quick wins. The client team responded by saying the client organization was too busy to work on this, as it already had a very full change program planned. One of the client Innovation Sponsors insisted the service provider team didn't need client input but instead should be using their own knowledge, judgment, and extensive experience to identify and develop potential ideas and bring these to the next meeting. The meeting closed.

In the first few weeks after the meeting, the service provider Innovation Leader began to develop a set of ideas, using various inputs, but struggled to make real progress to understand viability and potential business case without meaningful client input. In addition, there were issues in the Transformation change program and the service provider management team prioritized these above innovation development. For some time no additional progress was made on the innovation agenda.

Three months later, both parties agreed to skip the next scheduled Innovation Executive Governance meeting to enable all parties to focus on addressing challenges with and completing the delivery of the Transformation change program. During the next three months, the Transformation change program was completed and the service was handed over to Run Phase service teams to support.

Run Phase

Shortly before the next Innovation Executive Governance session was due to run, the service provider Innovation Sponsor reminded the Innovation Leader of the need to take a number of ideas to the next meeting. The Innovation Leader revisited the earlier work and, although concerned with the quality and depth of the items, a set of ideas were prepared ahead of the meeting.

The next scheduled Innovation Executive Governance meeting began with a lengthy discussion on issues in the Run service. Outside the meeting, the service provider had already recognized a number of issues and initiated a service improvement program. After 20 minutes, the client and service provider Innovation Sponsors agreed they should focus the remaining time on the innovation agenda, which was intended to focus on areas beyond the scope of service improvement. The service provider Innovation Leader walked through the initial set of ideas. The client team was not happy with these for a variety of reasons. They questioned the viability of some in the ideas due to specific nuances and previous history in its business and criticized other ideas for lack of detail. The meeting closed with the most senior client Innovation Sponsor and service provider Innovation Sponsor agreeing to have a one-to one-discussion to agree a better approach to innovation.

Following the Innovation Sponsors' discussion, the client appointed an Innovation Leader with a very good understanding of the business and a very good set of contacts. The service provider gave its own Innovation Leader more time to focus on innovation activities and both agreed to commit a small budget to select and move a small number of ideas forward.

Subsequently, the two Innovation Leaders worked together on a small number of jointly agreed items, running innovation workshops and follow on activities with business and technology experts from client and service provider organizations and, in some cases, additional third parties. A small number of ideas were assessed for viability and potential sponsorship and development work began on three of these. One in particular proved to have a very compelling business case for a project sponsor in the client's business. It also offered a potential opportunity for the service provider to grow its business with the client and both Innovation Leaders considered this a very strong potential win-win, which could only be delivered by a combination of the client's business knowledge and the service provider's domain-specific expertise.

The Innovation Leaders were empowered by the Innovation Sponsors not to wait for the next governance meeting to make progress, and the service provider invested to move three items forward to a point where they were ready to be jointly presented to the next Innovation Executive Governance meeting, and after which two would potentially be very quickly ready to make a commercial agreements on and hand over to program and change teams to implement.

Unfortunately, the beginning of the next scheduled Innovation Executive Governance meeting was dominated by client concerns about the quality of the Run Phase service. The most senior client sponsor for innovation stated wider joint innovation activity would now be halted, until the service provider could "get the basics right." The client moved its Innovation Leader to work on other nonrelated activities elsewhere in its business. The service provider gave its Innovation Leader a role in accelerating the service improvement program, which the client most definitely did not consider as "innovation" (for understandable reasons).

Subsequently, several months later, the Run service was greatly improved and the client sponsor agreed joint innovation activities should recommence. The client team was unable to reassign its original Innovation Leader to the role, due to the importance of the person's current assignment, and so a less-experienced member of the client team was assigned as client Innovation Leader.

The existing service provider Innovation Leader and the new client Innovation Leaders attempted to restart work on the three previous innovation items that had been placed on hold, including the item with the compelling business case. Although positive progress was made on one of the items, the client business sponsors for the other two potential innovations had not lost faith in the ability of the team to move these forward because of the delays in progress. The more junior client Innovation Leader also struggled to get client business input and buy-in into new potential idea and innovation development activity and the service provider Innovation Leader became frustrated with the lack of progress.

In the following Innovation Executive Governance meeting, the client and service provider Sponsors were clearly frustrated with the lack of progress. Both organizations began to blame each other. The client scored the service provider very lowly for innovation in both overall governance Set-Met ratings and in the service provider's annual Client Satisfaction surveys.

Summary

This was a deliberately lengthy example, blended from challenges within a number of client and service provider relationships. It highlights a number of key points:

- Joint innovation is built upon trust—the service provider must "earn the right" to develop an innovation agenda with a client— a solid Transformation Phase change program and effective Run Phase service are key for this.
- A partnership-based relationship will be required to enable successful joint innovation—the client cannot expect innovation

to be "done to them"—innovation in a client–service provider relationship is something which must be "done together" and have joint inputs to be successful.

- Innovation activity needs to start at the right time—but if it is delayed, there is a risk it will never start; if there are challenges in the relationship, the Transformation Phase change program or the Run Phase service, innovation activity at times can be focused on getting these issues right, before the scope is widened to other focus areas (whether this improvement activity is termed as innovation or not).

- Unless innovation is being focused on fixing issues and driving service improvement, innovation governance should be separated from the wider issues and challenges in the relationship—to enable the right level of focus (accepting that innovation is also dependent on getting the service and relationship basics right).

- For innovation to happen, someone must be responsible for driving it—in both client and service provider teams—and to be most effective the appointed Innovation Leaders must be leaders and influencers, with strong knowledge, interpersonal skills, and networks within and beyond their organizations.

- If innovation activity excites but then flounders, it will be very difficult to restart.

Successful Innovation Program in Financial Services Client

This is quite a different example to the previous one but it starts off in much the same way.

Engagement Phase

Following a highly competitive Engagement Phase, a client in a financial services industry and a service provider agreed a long-term services agreement. There was much discussion on "innovation" during the Engagement Phase, and a contract schedule was created.

- This described how both parties would appoint named Sponsors and Leaders for innovation and agree a detailed approach to joint governance during the Transformation Phase to prepare for an ongoing focus on joint innovation during the Run Phase.

- The agreed Transformation Phase change program and Run Phase service improvement activities were specifically excluded from innovation-related activities.
- The agreement agreed both parties would provide a budget for early stage innovation development activity.
- One specific initial focus area for innovation was included in the contract schedule—this set a significant (multimillion dollar) cost-saving target for the service provider to enable the client to achieve through innovation in a specific business function, outside the scope of the Transformation change program.

Joint Innovation Program

The two parties worked together through Transition and Transformation Phases. Both parties appointed an Innovation Leader: a part-time role in the client and a full-time role in the service provider. Both were well respected in their own organizations, had excellent networks and very good technical, business, commercial, and soft skills.

In parallel with the Transformation Phase change program, the two Innovation Leaders did two things. First, they worked together to establish how the two organizations would collaborate to manage, develop, and deliver innovation on an ongoing basis. Secondly they began work on the initial focus area set in the contract. They presented a recommended approach for both items at the first Innovation Executive Governance meeting, early in the Transformation Phase of the relationship. This was attended by senior Innovation Sponsor(s) from both parties. The recommendations were well received and the Innovation Leaders were tasked with moving forward in both areas.

The client was a global organization, which had rapidly grown through merger and acquisition activity. It was effectively a federated organization, made up of a number of large country and regional financial services companies. In many cases, each business unit still operated independently of the others. Group operations strategy was to move to globally based business processes and functions, where appropriate, to achieve efficiencies through economies of scale and use of best practice.

Reviewing the initial focus area for innovation, the Innovation Leaders quickly identified the potential for significant cost savings by use of emerging technologies and standardization around best practices. There were, however, significant challenges as key stakeholders wished to retain local control of their functions. Using part of their innovation development budget, the two Innovation Leaders undertook a series of activities to better understand the current state, working with client business experts and domain subject matter experts from within the service provider's global organization. This was followed by a series of global and regional innovation workshops to identify and develop opportunities, challenges, and ideas for innovation. This was very well received by the local business units, and the local stakeholders began to buy into the innovation approach.

A good deal of detailed work and analysis followed. The two Innovation Leaders funded the time of client and service provider subject matter experts to develop and assess a set of viable innovations that could be applied to achieve significant cost savings. These consisted of a series of new technology implementations and, in some cases, global deployment of existing local best practices. The innovations developed were a combination of new to the world innovations and a mixture of new to the organization and new to business unit innovations. The Innovation Leaders worked together to qualify the potential savings from applying these innovations, balanced against costs of development and deployment.

The business case developed exceeded the targets set in the contract, and sponsorship for a major change project was agreed in the client. The recommendations were reviewed with the client and service provider Innovation Sponsors, and it was agreed a global change project should be initiated, staffed by the client's standard project teams, and supplemented by domain subject matter expertise in the service provider, to enable new technologies to be further developed, tested, and configured for use in the client's business environment.

The Innovation Leaders kept a watching brief on the change project, with regular reviews. The change project was highly successful and the benefits realization review quantified cost savings significantly above those initially targeted. The project won a major award in the client organization for "Best Global Project." The Innovation Leaders were commended for their role in the development of the ideas and innovation deployed by the change project.

In parallel to the above activity, the Innovation Leaders created a gated joint innovation management process, focused on addressing a series of innovation themes (areas important to the client's business). Each theme was broken down to identify key challenges and opportunities and ideas generated from the client and service provider teams to address them. Each idea taken forward was developed and qualified, and a sponsor confirmed should the capability and business case be considered viable. Focus areas included video analytics, queue busting, cashless payments, and energy usage reduction. Many items were progressed from idea through to delivery and a series of significant business benefits achieved by the client. The service provider also benefitted through increased business from some (not all) of the delivered innovations. The client consistently measured the value of innovation from the service provider as Exceeded in governance Set-Met targets and formal Client Satisfaction surveys.

Summary

This example highlights the high value which can be achieved through joint innovation activities developed using a *by design* approach, with strong sponsorship, leadership, funding, and input from both client and service provider teams.

Successful Retail Client Innovation Project

In the next example, a client and service provider had an existing service relationship but had not previously discussed or focused on achieving value through joint innovation.

Introduction

A retail client had an existing relationship with a larger service provider. Initial focus had been placed on the initial Transformation Phase change program, which was now complete. Although from time to time there were challenges with the Run Phase service, overall the client was happy with the performance of the service provider.

The overall business of the client organization was becoming increasingly focused on driving innovation for and with its retail customers, as a means of differentiating itself from the competition, retaining and growing business with existing customers, and gaining new ones. The client organization externally hired a new business unit leader for the business unit that owned the relationship with the service provider. In line with the overall business, the new business unit leader considered successful innovation within the business unit and for the wider business as a key priority. Effectively, this person became the client Innovation Sponsor.

The service provider organization also considered driving innovation for and with its clients as a priority for the same reasons as the client. The service provider account team was keen to develop opportunities with the client for joint innovation. Effectively, the service provider's leader for the client account became the service provider Innovation Sponsor.

The leadership teams of the client business unit and service provider met and discussed in detail the need to drive joint innovation activity, which should focus on using the differentiating capabilities of the wider service provider's organization to address priority challenges and opportunities in the client's business. It was agreed, rather than to spread this activity too widely to begin with, innovation would be focused on one key priority focus area, aligned with the client's business priorities. The selected focus area for innovation was based on enabling the client to gain a better understanding of its online retail customers, to drive a more personalized relationship with them.

In parallel to the client engaging with a team of retail subject matter experts from the service provider's wider organization, the client and service provider agreed to run a joint innovation project to very quickly create a new capability, to showcase how the organizations could work together to develop and deliver innovation.

The two parties agreed to use one of the service provider's cross-client innovation programs for this. The program assigns a team of top talent student interns, supported by experienced mentors, to work with a client on a specific challenge or opportunity and tasks them with creating a differentiating new prototype capability in a matter of weeks along with a supporting white paper demonstrating how the prototype can be taken forward and made into a live capability. Apart from client subject matter expert inputs, the project was funded by the service provider.

Although there was also many other joint innovation activities between the client and service provider, focused on both incremental changes to the services and wider more transformative innovation, this example focuses on this project as a very tangible example of what can be achieved when two organizations determine to develop and deliver innovation *by design*.

Innovation Project

The service provider appointed an experienced Innovation Leader to be lead mentor for the project. The Innovation Leader worked with the client Sponsors and wider client stakeholders to develop an innovation challenge centered on the client's business priority of creating a more personalized customer relationship. The challenge was worded in such a way to enable the assigned team to innovate on the requirements in addition to the solution to be developed. The client appointed an Innovation Leader to lead client input into the project.

The student interns had a mixture of technical and business skills but were totally new to the client and the retail industry, apart from the experience we all have as retail customers. They were given an induction and spent some time thinking around the challenge, before visiting the client's head office, where they were given a sheep dip into the client's business, priorities, and details of the challenge. An initial innovation workshop was facilitated by the service provider Innovation Leader between the client and service provider teams, from which the interns developed a long list of ideas.

In the next week, the interns reduced the long list to three specific ideas, each of which they developed further. A second innovation workshop was run at one of the service provider's technology labs. During this the interns presented the three worked ideas to the client team, who selected a favorite. They were very impressed with the selected idea, as it was a totally new concept, which their business had not considered and was not in use by any of their competition.

Over the next eight weeks, the interns, supported by the client and service provider Innovation Leaders, had access to a range of client and service provider subject matter experts and resources. They collaborated closely with the client business team to develop and iteratively improve a rich working prototype of their solution so that it could actively be demonstrated and used by trial users. This was then showcased to many people in the client organization at a major innovation event at the client's head office.

The client Innovation Sponsor and wider team were delighted with the idea and prototype created. The client used it internally and externally as a showcase of what focused innovation could achieve. The client and service provider were jointly nominated and won an external award for the innovation. The client gained significant business value and used the project's output as a valuable input into the strategic work to develop an enhanced personalized customer experience. The service provider benefited through improvements in client satisfaction and being viewed as an innovation partner by the client, key inputs into eventual extension of the service contract and wider business growth between the client and service provider, as part of a wider joint focus on the innovation agenda. The project also helped to firmly establish and cement an ongoing innovation relationship between the two organizations, which has continued and includes a series of high value partnership-related activities, focused on service improvement and evolution and on wider business differentiating innovations.

Summary

This example highlights the significant value that clients and service providers can achieve through joint innovation activities, by taking a focused and structured approach to innovation management, development, and delivery, utilizing the respective strengths and capabilities of the client and service provider organizations.

CHAPTER 7

Innovation Evolution

Introduction

By definition, innovation isn't something which stands still. There are always new things to learn and new ways in which clients and service providers can work together to achieve ever more successful outcomes from driving collaborative innovation throughout the life cycle of their relationships.

When developing this publication, I wanted to share some of the newer things out there, which have made a significant impact in recent times and will continue to do so in the future. As I was thinking about this, I was aware there were so many items I could include but I've made a decision to focus on three.

I've seen clients and service providers use each of these items, often in combination, to very good advantage. Of course, none of these are totally new to the world any longer but they will be relatively new or even totally new to some people and some organizations working in both clients and service providers, and so I believe each is very worthy of highlighting.

Yes, there are other many items but we can't cover everything, and if there is a follow-on edition of this book, the great news is there will be new ones too! For now though, these are the three items I wish to highlight:

- Design Thinking
- Digital Innovation Platforms
- Joint Innovation Culture

Areas for Innovation

Design Thinking	Digital Innovation Platforms	Joint Innovation Culture

The following sections outline each of these three areas.

Design Thinking

The concept of Design Thinking isn't new. At its heart, Design Thinking is a mechanism for improving problem solving and solution development by focusing on the needs of the end user and end user outcomes, rather than features and functions. Empathy and understanding of end user and sponsor's objectives and needs are vitally important. Often in the past, Design Thinking approaches have primarily been applied to enhancing new product development and, of course, in recent years to mobile app development. However, as I have directly witnessed, Design Thinking can also be a fantastic mechanism for developing and delivering ideas and innovation in a wide range of ways in a service context.

The details around Design Thinking are well documented elsewhere. For example, IBM's own approach, IBM Design Thinking, is highlighted on the IBM website (http://www.ibm.com/design/thinking/) and through a great series of YouTube videos, but I've included a few thoughts of my own here for those less familiar with the concept. My recommendation is to have a quick read of this and then follow it up with your own much more in-depth research of how you can apply Design Thinking approaches within your own context.

IBM views Design Thinking in terms of three key principles:

1. A focus on user outcomes
2. Restless reinvention
3. Use of diverse empowered teams

It's easy to see the value of these principles in a services context.

1. A focus on user outcomes—concentrate design and improvement of the service not on the technology and business widgets but on

the outcomes from the perspective of those who use the service—it sounds so obvious but ask yourself, is this always the case?

2. Restless reinvention—maintain a continuous dialogue and feedback loop with the users, both when developing and changing the services they use and beyond to identify and develop ideas of how the service can be further improved—so it is a great mechanism for generating new ideas and innovations plus service improvement innovations.

3. Use of diverse empowered teams—diverse teams result in better results; when a client and service provider team really work together to focus on a service improvement idea or a wider innovation, the whole of their combined knowledge and skills is much greater than the parts—I'd add to this the use of a wide range of idea sources as outlined in Chapter Five.

Design Thinking and IBM's own variant, IBM Design Thinking, come with a whole series of approaches and techniques for identifying and evaluating ideas, iteratively developing and assessing the viability of prototype innovations, and so on. These can be invaluable if effectively applied in a client–service provider relationship context. Examples include the following:

- Engagement Phase—service provider application of Design Thinking to better understand the wants and needs of the client sponsors and users
- Transformation Phase—client and service provider joint application of Design Thinking to create or change one or more services focused on end users and user outcomes
- Run Phase—client and service provider joint application of Design Thinking for ongoing service improvement innovation focused on end users and user outcomes (or simply service improvement if the client does not consider service improvement to be innovation!) and/or for wider scope innovation activity focused on end users and user outcomes

If you are a client or a service provider and not already familiar with Design Thinking, or if it is not currently actively applied in your service relationship, I'd strongly recommend further research. Read a few of the many summary write-ups available online on the topic, view some of the video demonstrations of how it's been applied, and perhaps follow up in more detail via books and subject matter experts.

If, as I believe will be the case, you quickly recognize the value, discuss it in your own organization and with your clients or service providers and drive initial pilot usage of some of the approaches and techniques. The great thing is you don't need to apply them all. You can pick and choose what will be most useful in the context of what you are doing. If you try it out, I believe you'll recognize the value and keep on doing it and, most importantly, the end users of the services will recognize the value too. The initial services you design, the service improvements you apply, and wider innovations you jointly develop with be of a higher quality and drive better outcomes for the end users of the service.

Digital Innovation Platforms

A few years ago, one of the challenges with many early stage innovation opportunities was the need to invest in and wait for IT infrastructure to be set up as a platform to develop, test, and deploy the innovation onto. The advent of public, private, and hybrid cloud computing capabilities, of course, has addressed this for many organizations today.

Even then, there are often challenges in building new IT applications from scratch and so on. Building upon the cloud delivery approach, digital innovation platforms provide a great base for fast development and delivery of innovation, particularly when used in conjunction with a Design Thinking approach to iteratively develop and improve applications and services.

A digital innovation platform is at its heart simply an IT platform for developing, running, and managing apps and services. The one I know best is based upon IBM Bluemix, and so I've centered my explanation and recommendations in this section around this but the text holds true for any similar solutions and capabilities.

IBM Bluemix includes an open standards, cloud platform for developing, running, and managing applications and services. The platform can be used to host and manage apps but I've focused here on the innovation angle. This is effectively the ability to take a new idea and use it to very quickly develop new capabilities, without the need to commission IT servers and storage and reusing many existing application and application system support services, rather than recreating or installing them each time. These applications and services are made available from a catalog of IBM, third party, and open source services. Application programming interfaces can be easily used to tap into a client organization's existing applications data and services and service provider and additional third-party applications and services. You get the idea.

In effect, when developing a new application, only the new elements require to be developed. Virtually everything else can be tapped into using the innovation platform. In the extreme, such platforms can be used for non-developers to build new applications using a plug-and-play style approach.

During the early stages of the innovation management process, digital innovation platforms are ideal for quickly and cost effectively creating prototype applications, showcasing them to sponsors and end users, understanding refinements needed, and quickly and iteratively making changes and updates.

In a client–service provider relationship, digital innovation platforms can also be used as a mechanism for integrating new capabilities with existing client, service provider, and third-party applications and data sources, during the joint innovation management and execution process.

I'm aware of IBM's work, for example, with one banking client, who was perhaps skeptical of the claims around digital innovation platforms and tasked IBM to create a new prototype capability from a range of five options in a week. The IBM team used Bluemix to create prototype capabilities for all five options, delighting the client.

This example highlights the power of digital innovation platforms to make a huge difference, particularly on the early stages of joint innovation development between a client and service provider and when used in conjunction with Design Thinking for fast iterative solution development focused on end service user outcomes.

Joint Innovation Culture

This is perhaps an intangible idea to many people but I believe it can be hugely important, particularly if a joined up focus on and culture of innovation is built between a client and its service providers.

So, what is an innovation culture? As with the word "innovation" itself, there are lots of potential definitions out there but I'd got with this simple one: "An innovation culture supports and encourages new ideas, creative thinking and change which generates new or improved products, services or processes."

In the context of a client–service provider relationship, this can be very much focused on identifying and delivering on opportunities for ongoing service improvement for the client and/or wider joint innovation activity between the client and service provider. To be successful, the "innovation culture" needs to encompass end users of the service, supporting client and service provider teams and potentially a wider ecosystem.

It should be no surprise that the three key enablers for achieving a joint innovation culture described below are very much repeated in the chapter focused on Recommendations.

Leadership and Enabling Support from the Top

Leaders in the client and service provider organizations need to clearly articulate innovation is important, but more than that they need to sponsor innovation activities and enable the organization to practically make the changes needed for innovation to really be part of everybody's job role, in a tangible way by empowering their employees, as detailed below.

Innovation from Everyone

Employees in client and service providers should understand innovation is a priority for their organization and partner organizations, but this needs to be made tangible and real to them. One of the best ways of doing this is by directly getting their input into the front end of the innovation management (and/or service improvement) process.

Employees should be given time on a regular basis to take a step back and think about how the service could be improved and identify ideas for wider innovation. I fully understand this can be a tough task in cost conscious service agreements but enabling such an approach will pay dividends for the client and the service provider. During my time working with the UK National Outsourcing Association, I saw a fantastic example of this in one organization, whose core team and number of employees were quite small as they effectively procured most of what their business needed from a range of service providers. This organization ensured every service agreement included a mechanism to make the above happen and proactively worked with their service providers to deliver current selected ideas and innovations and identify the next set. My recommendation for client organizations is to think about the value of such an approach and work with your service providers to build something into your agreements for this during the Engagement Phase.

Ongoing idea box systems can be useful but only if the ideas posted are assessed, worked on, some taken through the innovation process, the benefits of delivered innovations communicated, and, hopefully, those responsible for delivered ideas rewarded.

I'm a bigger fan of running regularly scheduled focused innovation sessions or events, set against a framework of business priorities and specific challenges and opportunities. For example, an innovation challenge of "How can we improve and deliver great customer service in the store?" focuses minds on this particular business priority. These events can be face to face, virtual or online.

Skills will also be important. Once again, we can think of the ideal skills profile for innovation and collaboration activities in terms of T- and TT-shaped professionals, bringing together deep domain and specialist knowledge with a wider skill set covering communications, empathy, collaboration, and so on.

I'm also very keen on getting people to generate and discuss ideas, with the support of an experienced facilitator. Design Thinking techniques will really help here. Getting diverse teams together really does generally generate better results, so why not hold quarterly sessions, where end users and client and service provider support teams and whatever third-party subject matter experts you need get together in a room or use online capabilities to generate and develop ideas? After all, not all the smart people work for either the client or service provider. And this is a relatively low-cost approach. The sessions could be face-to-face, online, or both. They just need to be prepared, executed, and followed up effectively by engaged and engaging Innovation Leaders, empowered by Innovation Sponsors in the client and service provider organizations.

This type of approach will make the "innovation" word tangible to teams in both client and service provider alike. It generates a fantastic front end for the joint innovation management and execution process. Once this is done, it's what you do next which will matter, that is, putting in place and running joint innovation governance and joint innovation management and execution to take the best ideas forward, develop them into viable capabilities with solid business cases, and deliver upon them.

The Power of Positive Communications

So, the executives are now making innovation a priority, the employees in both client and service provider are being given a little time and actively encouraged and supported to identify and develop ideas, and innovation leadership is in place to drive a joint innovation management and execution process to take the best ideas forward and ensure they are delivered. What else?

- Communicate innovation as a priority—in executive briefings, team meetings, and so on
- Communicate innovation progress—which ideas have been taken forward, from where and why
- Communicate and celebrate innovation success—tell client and service provider employees which innovations have been delivered, articulate the value and benefits derived (the message may be slightly different in the client and service provider), reward client and service provider employees who came up with the ideas that have driven value, reward the teams which delivered them, put the best ones up for external awards, and celebrate success

By doing all these things, the employees in client and service provider will understand what innovation is, see the benefits and be keen to get involved. There may even be a buzz about the place. You've developed an innovation culture that supports and encourages new ideas, creative thinking, and change that is generating new or improved products, services, or processes.

CHAPTER 8

Recommendations

Introduction

This chapter builds upon the contents of the earlier chapters to address client and service provider challenges and make a set of detailed recommendations for both clients and service providers at key stages during the life cycle of their service relationship. The objective is to enable clients and service providers to achieve successful and sustainable joint innovation *by design*.

The recommendations have been split into four parts.

1. Engagement—the first part includes a series of recommendations for both clients and service providers before and during the Engagement Phase, that is, when the client is looking to find the right service partner and the service provider is looking to win a service contract.
2. Transformation—the second part focuses on recommended actions for clients and service providers when establishing a new service relationship. Typically, these actions will be carried out during the Transformation Phase.
3. Run in new service relationships—the third part summarizes recommended actions for clients and service providers to set up, run, and govern an ongoing joint innovation execution process during the Run Phase of a new service relationship.
4. Run in existing service relationships—the fourth part considers what clients and service providers should do when already in the Run Phase of an established service relationship, which to date either hasn't had a focus on innovation or, if there has been such a focus, it has not been successful.

Client Recommendations are as follows:

Phase	Recommendation
Engagement	Pre-Engagement Planning—Understand what innovation is, whether it is needed and, if so, where it should be focused
	Pre-Engagement Planning—Consider optimum innovation approach
	Service Provider Engagement and Selection—Ensure innovation is planned for *by design*
Transformation	Agree and establish innovation governance with the service provider
	Work with the service provider to develop and deliver agreed Transformation Phase innovation deliverables
	Establish a joint innovation culture with the service provider
Run (New)	Work with the service provider to develop and run a Joint Innovation Management and Execution process
	Deliver quick-win innovations
	Manage innovation governance with the service provider
Run (Existing—No Previous Innovation Focus)	Review motivations
	Develop joint innovation as if in a new relationship
Run (Existing—Innovation not Working)	Take a step back
	Begin again—develop joint innovation as if in a new relationship

Service Provider Recommendations are as follows:

Phase	Recommendation
Engagement	Develop a strategic approach for delivering innovation with your clients
	Client Engagement—Understand what the client really wants in terms of innovation
	Client Engagement—Ensure innovation is planned for *by design*
Transformation	Agree and establish innovation governance with the client
	Work with the client to develop and deliver agreed Transformation Phase innovation deliverables
	Establish a joint innovation culture with the client

(Continued)

Phase	Recommendation
Run (New)	Work with the client to develop and run a Joint Innovation Management and Execution process
	Deliver quick-win innovations
	Manage innovation governance with the client
Run (Existing—No Previous Innovation Focus)	Review motivations
	Develop joint innovation as if in a new relationship
Run (Existing— Innovation Not Working)	Take a step back
	Begin again—develop joint innovation as if in a new relationship

The recommendations are intended to be used in conjunction with the contents and learning from the earlier Chapters, including Chapter Five—Innovation *by Design*. It should be noted that the publication is not intended to be an overarching framework for successfully setting up and delivering a service-based relationship in a wider context, as the focus is primarily on enabling successful joint innovation. Although for this to be achieved, the relationship will need to be in a positive place. On the converse side, in many cases the recommendations made will help foster a more positive overall relationship and, in particular, enable clients to get greater value from the relationship with their service providers.

The primary intention of this chapter and the wider book is to concentrate on what needs to be done by clients and service providers alike to ensure innovation is successfully developed and delivered during the lifetime of their service relationship in a collaborative and ongoing basis *by design* to achieve value and benefits for the client and the service provider.

Part One—Engagement Phase

This section documents recommendations for client and service provider organizations when entering into and progressing an engagement to agree and contract for a new service relationship, with a focus on ensuring the right enablers are in place for achieving successful and sustainable joint innovation between the organizations during the lifetime of the contract, once agreed.

The section has been split into two subsections, one focused on the client and one focused on the service provider.

Client recommendations include the following:

1. Pre-Engagement Planning—Understand what innovation is, whether it is needed and, if so, where it should be focused
2. Pre-Engagement Planning—Consider optimum innovation approach
3. Service Provider Engagement and Selection—Ensure innovation is planned for *by design*

Service provider recommendations include the following:

1. Develop a strategic approach for delivering innovation with your clients
2. Client Engagement—Understand what the client really wants in terms of innovation
3. Client Engagement—Ensure innovation is planned for *by design*

Client Recommendations

Recommendation One—Pre-Engagement Planning—Understand what innovation is, whether it is needed and, if so, where it should be focused

During Pre-Engagement Phase planning for a new service agreement, in terms of innovation, I recommend the client organization ask themselves four key questions:

1. What will innovation mean in the context of the service relationship?
2. Do we really want or need any innovation from the selected service provider at all?
3. What is the scope of innovation we want the selected service provider to deliver during the service relationship?
4. Where do we want to focus innovation activity with the selected service provider?

These questions appear simple and straight forward but from experience many client organizations do not consider some or all of them. By reviewing and answering these questions, a client organization can make a very solid start. Let's look at each of these questions in more detail.

What Will Innovation Mean in the Context of the Service Relationship?

Some client organizations may already have an organization wide or business unit definition of what innovation means. If so, link to this and work with it to see how it can be tailored to work in the context of the planned service agreement. If such a definition does not exist, create one which will work in the context of the proposed service. In Chapter Five, in the Agree Approach section, a number of example potential definitions for innovation in a service context are outlined but you must develop the one that works best for your own organization and context.

In case this sounds like a purely theoretical exercise, here is a simple example. A client organization is planning to begin a tender for a new IT service agreement and develops a definition for innovation in the context of the service agreement as follows: "Innovation is the application of new and emerging technologies developed by the service provider to enable the client's business to increase revenue, reduce cost and/or improve customer service ratings."

In this example, the client may subsequently agree with the service provider that a number of new and emerging technologies should be delivered during the Transformation Phase and/or new ones introduced over time during the Run Phase. By assigning a clear business outcome to the innovation (increased revenue, reduced cost, and/or improved customer service ratings), the impact of the innovation activity becomes measurable.

By using the definition above, the client organization will understand what innovation is and be able to tell when they're getting it or not getting it from their service provider. Equally, the service provider will also have a clear indication and understand the business outcomes that must be achieved. For instance, in the example above, in the future the client and service provider will have a clear view that innovation should be about implementing the service provider's new and emerging technologies, when the business case to do so is aligned with the stated outcomes. If this is achieved, it will be counted as innovation in the context of the service relationship.

Do We Really Want or Need Any Innovation from the Selected Service Provider at All?

If is, of course, possible when attempting to answer this question, that innovation does not appear to be relevant in the context of the intended service relationship. Perhaps the selected service provider will deliver Q widgets at a price of P and this won't really change over time, and the only "innovation" required from the service provider will be to cut its price. In this case, it's perfectly reasonable to be realistic and consider innovation is simply not relevant to this specific service relationship. At least, you've made a conscious decision not to include any focus on innovation.

Even if this is the case, I still have one recommendation to make. Depending on the service provider selected, consider if it will still be possible for your organization to gain additional value from the relationship by tapping into the wider capabilities of the service provider, by linking this explicitly or implicitly to the service relationship. For example, if the service provider has wider capabilities very relevant for your organization and/or industry, it would make sense to use the service relationship as a means of getting preferential access to these.

On a very positive note, for many service relationships the client will see a clear advantage from focusing on innovation with their service provider. This may be in the initial Transformation Phase, as an effective mechanism for ongoing service improvement in the Run Phase and/or as a means of tapping into the service provider's wider capabilities to gain additional business value.

What Is the Scope of Innovation We Want the Selected Service Provider to Deliver During the Service Relationship?

Assuming a level of innovation from the service provider is desirable, the next action is to consider the scope of innovation required.

As outlined in Chapter Five, areas of scope can include the following:

- Innovation purely within the scope of the contracted services during the Transformation Phase
- Innovation purely within the scope of the contracted services during the Run Phase delivered as service improvement (noting that some clients do not consider service improvement as innovation)

- Wider innovation within specific business units of the client
- Wider innovation across the entire business organization of the client

The client should consider if innovation is desired purely within the scope of contracted service or whether wider above-service contract innovation with the service provider may also be desirable. If so, then this may also have implications for the wider procurement and contracting process, as the client may wish to identify and verify the key wider capabilities and attributes of an ideal service provider and include these as a weighting factor in the overall service provider selection process.

Where do We Want to Focus Innovation Activity with the Selected Service Provider?

If the client has determined the scope for innovation is purely within the scope of the contracted services, the answer to this question may be relatively simple. If the scope of the service is large, then the client may identify specific areas that need to be addressed during the Transformation Phase. Equally, there may be one or more obvious focus areas for ongoing service improvement in the Run Phase. By thinking these through during Pre-Engagement Phase planning, the client will be well positioned to work with potential service providers during Engagement phase.

If the client has determined the scope for innovation includes wider above-service contract innovation, then it will be very useful for the client, even at this early stage, to identify initial focus areas for wider innovation, aligned with the client's business priorities.

The Proof Points described in Chapter Six include an example where a financial services client identified a business priority for wider scope innovation to work on with its service provider and included this as a contracted innovation action for the selected service provider. Many client organizations may not wish to include such activity, as they may consider it could deflect focus from the primary objectives of implementing and supporting core services but for larger scope and scale service agreements this can be a good mechanism for creating a tangible mechanism for achieving additional value from the service provider through innovation at a relatively early stage of the relationship.

Using business prioritized focus areas for wider innovation can also be a good method for helping to select the most appropriate service provider. For example, if there is little differentiation between the service providers in terms of the main requirements of the service contract, understanding which service provider is most likely to deliver most value from wider innovation activity can be used as an additional assessment consideration.

Recommendation Two—Pre-Engagement Planning—Consider optimum innovation approach

Once the client organization understands what innovation should mean in the context of the service relationship, along with the scope and priority focus areas for innovation, before engaging potential service providers, it is recommended that the client consider what its ideal approach would be for driving joint innovation with its service provider.

Items to consider here include the following:

1. Who in the client organization will sponsor innovation activities with the service provider?
2. Who in the client organization will lead innovation activities with the service provider on the ground, both during the Transformation Phase and the Run Phase?
3. How will innovation activities with the service provider be funded?
4. How will innovation activities with the service provider be governed?
5. How will innovation activities with the service provider be practically developed, delivered, and managed?
6. What are the targets for innovation activities with the service provider and can they be quantified at this early stage?
7. How will innovation activities with the service provider be measured?
8. Should/how should innovation with the service provider be included in the service contract?
9. What will the service provider need to do to convince the client of its capability to deliver innovation in the context of the service agreement? This should include capabilities within the scope of the service agreement and if wider scope innovation is sought, specific relevant additional capabilities.

10. What culture does a service provider require to deliver innovation collaboratively with the client organization and potentially third parties?

The recommendation at this stage is not to spend a huge amount of time developing detailed answers to each question but instead to consider the questions and begin developing a view on potential answers. The intention is for the client to have developed a view of what is really needed to drive successful innovation in the context of the service relationship, ready to use this during the Engagement Phase.

If a third-party adviser organization has been contracted to manage, assist, and/or input into the Engagement Phase, it is also recommended to review the above questions with the adviser and agree how innovation will be best considered and assessed during the Engagement Phase.

Recommendation Three—Service Provider Engagement and Selection—Ensure innovation is planned for by design

In general, once the Engagement Phase begins for proper, strict rules will be enforced to manage interactions between the client and bidding service providers. It is strongly recommend RFI, RFP, and similar documents include sections explaining the client's position and requirements for innovation (developed from the considerations outlined above). Specific questions can also be included requesting service providers to indicate how they will meet the client's requirements, demonstrating proof points to verify their capabilities and articulating how they've delivered innovation with similar client organizations in the same or a similar industry, with tangible examples of approach, outcomes, and benefits.

Once a short list of service providers has been agreed and detailed face-to-face discussions and meetings begin, the same considerations should be reviewed in more detail.

As part of final service provider selection processes, often very detailed discussions are held. When considering innovation, these should include the following Agree Approach activities, as detailed earlier in Chapter Five.

1. Agree Innovation Definition
2. Agree Innovation Scope
3. Agree Initial Innovation Focus Areas
4. Agree Innovation Leadership
5. Agree Innovation Sponsorship
6. Agree Funding Mechanism(s)
7. Agree Manage Governance Approach—including target setting and measurement
8. Agree Joint Innovation Execution Approach

If the client team followed the recommendations above, they will have a good idea of what will be needed to meet their innovation-related requirements. The recommendation here is to sit down with potential service provider teams, review and agree in detail how this will work in practice, and make an assessment of whether the service provider really has the capability, motivation, and culture to successfully deliver innovation to meet your requirements.

A key question I have often been asked is whether to contract or not to contract for innovation. Obviously, if there is a specific innovation commitment that needs to be delivered during the Transformation Phase change program, this should be carefully contracted for. In terms of a mechanism for driving wider ongoing innovation, in all honesty I am sometimes a little ambivalent.

In favor, I have witnessed great examples of innovation contract schedules setting out a practical framework for the joint management, development, and delivery of innovation, which have subsequently been followed through and used to drive real success. Equally, I have seen great success when no contract schedule for innovation is in place, but both client and service provider organizations have developed a culture of nurturing and delivering innovation and put in place the sponsorship, leadership, funding, resources, and process to make it happen.

On the flip side, I've experienced great innovation contract schedules which have then been largely ignored by client, service provider, or both, as the Engagement Phase teams have walked away and the Run Phase teams on one or both sides have lacked the capability and/or motivation to make innovation really happen. Carefully considering what the client organization's real needs are for innovation and engaging with potential service providers to agree how this will work in practice is very important but it is not a replacement for ensuring both client and service providers are motivated to work together to manage, develop, and deliver innovation during Transformation and Run Phases. Successful innovation needs sponsorship, leadership, funding, resources, and process to make it happen consistently and successful joint innovation needs this from both parties.

On balance though, I do recommend the client agrees a framework contract schedule with the service provider during the Engagement Phase to detail and agree how innovation will be governed, managed, developed, delivered, and funded but this needs to be designed in such a way to include a level of flexibility. It must enable both parties to work together to meet the evolving needs of the client and also consider what is in it for the service provider too. The framework should include outcome-based targets for the initial time period of the service agreement and, particularly for longer term agreements, a mechanism for setting new joint outcome-based targets over time, which reflect and match the evolution of the client's business priorities and the service provider's evolving capabilities.

Service Provider Recommendations

Recommendation One—Develop a strategic approach for delivering innovation with your clients

This recommendation is not linked to engagement with a specific client but instead focused on how service providers should be developing a thought through and supported approach for delivering innovation for and with their portfolio of service clients.

This needs to encompass each of the potential scope areas for innovation. The service provider must have at least a considered approach for developing and delivering innovation in the scope of the core services contract during the Transformation Phase and in terms of incremental service improvement innovation during the Run Phase. Many service providers will also wish to develop an approach for being able to deliver wider scope innovation for their clients, beyond the core services contract. This can be an important mechanism for delivering additional value to the client from the service relationship and as a means of developing significant additional business opportunities with the client for the service provider. Such an approach can be a key differentiator for the service provider.

In terms of what should be included in the service provider's strategic approach for innovation, the focus and content will vary greatly across service providers, but the key aspects that need to be developed will include sponsorship, leadership, funding, resourcing, business models, staff motivation, targets, measurement, and content focus areas for delivering innovation with service clients. If the service provider has a clear strategic approach for these areas, it will be in a strong position to differentiate itself during the Engagement Phase, satisfy its clients, and grow business during Transformation and Run Phases.

Recommendation Two—Client Engagement—Understand what the client really wants in terms of innovation

I hesitated a little when wording this recommendation as it appears so obvious but this is all about empathy. There is an opportunity here to consider and use a number of Design Thinking approaches and techniques to better understand what the client really wants in terms of innovation (and beyond).

The core of this recommendation is to understand what the clients view as and want, in terms of innovation, in the context of the service relationship. Are they looking for innovation within the core scope of the service contract only? What innovation do they need in the Transformation Phase change program? What is their view on service improvement? Are they looking for a service provider who can also offer wider value by supporting innovation activity beyond the core scope of the service?

This can be difficult in the early stages of an engagement, when the primary contact between the client and service provider is through formal responses to RFI, RFP, and similar documents, but generally there are opportunities to raise questions and gain greater insights.

Once the above is understood, it will be significantly easier for the service providers to understand what capabilities they will need and which areas they need to focus on with the clients in terms of innovation to differentiate themselves and help to win the deal in the Engagement Phase and to satisfy and delight the clients during Transformation and Run Phases.

Recommendation Three—Client Engagement—Ensure innovation is planned for by design

Once a short list of service providers has been agreed and detailed face-to-face discussions and meetings begin, the client's wants and needs should be reviewed in more detail. Again the service provider should listen to the client and use what it learns to hone its approach on innovation for the specific client, highlighting its capabilities, motivation, and proof points.

Many client organizations may not be well versed in the importance of managing, developing, and delivering innovation *by design* with their service providers, and the service provider may need to assist the client to develop its thinking in this area (in addition to recommending the client purchases one or more copies of this publication!).

As part of final service provider selection processes, often very detailed discussions are held. When considering innovation, these should include the following Agree Approach activities, as detailed earlier in Chapter Five.

1. Agree Innovation Definition
2. Agree Innovation Scope
3. Agree Initial Innovation Focus Areas
4. Agree Innovation Leadership
5. Agree Innovation Sponsorship
6. Agree Funding Mechanism(s)
7. Agree Manage Governance Approach—including target setting and measurement
8. Agree Joint Innovation Execution Approach

The recommendation here is to sit down with the client team, review and agree in detail how this will work in practice, and highlight how, as a service provider, your organization really does have the capability, motivation, and culture to successfully deliver innovation in line with the client's requirements.

A key question I have often been asked is whether to contract or not to contract for innovation. Obviously, if there is a specific innovation commitment that needs to be delivered during the Transformation Phase change program, this should be carefully contracted for. In terms of a mechanism for driving wider ongoing innovation, in all honesty I am sometimes a little ambivalent.

In favor, I have witnessed great examples of innovation contract schedules setting out a practical framework for the joint management, development, and delivery of innovation, which have subsequently been followed through and used to drive real success. Equally, I have seen great success when no contract schedule for innovation is in place, but both client and service provider organizations have developed a culture of nurturing and delivering innovation and put in place the sponsorship, leadership, funding, resources, and process to make it happen.

On the flip side, I've experienced great innovation contract schedules that have then been largely ignored by client, service provider, or both, as the Engagement Phase teams have walked away and the Run Phase teams on one or both sides have lacked the capability and/or motivation to make innovation really happen. Carefully considering what the client organization's real needs are for innovation and engaging with the client to agree how this will work in practice is very important but it is not a replacement for ensuring both client and service providers are motivated to work together to manage, develop, and deliver innovation during Transformation and Run Phases. Successful innovation needs sponsorship, leadership, funding, resources, and process to make it happen consistently and successful joint innovation needs this from both parties.

On balance though, I do recommend the client agrees a framework contract schedule with the service provider during the Engagement Phase to detail and agree how innovation will be governed, managed, developed, delivered, and funded but this needs to be designed in such a way to include a level of flexibility. It must enable both parties to work together to meet the evolving needs of the client—also consider what is in it for the service provider too. The framework should include outcome-based targets for the initial time period of the service agreement and, particularly for longer term agreements, a mechanism for setting new joint outcome-based targets over time, which reflect and match the evolution of the client's business priorities and the service provider's evolving capabilities.

Part Two—Transformation Phase

This section documents recommendations for client and service provider organizations during the Transformation Phase of a contract for a new service relationship, with a focus on setting up governance for management, development, and delivery of innovation and joint innovation execution of agreed Transformation Phase innovation-related deliverables.

The section has been split into two subsections, one focused on the client and one focused on the service provider.

Client recommendations include the following:

1. Agree and establish innovation governance with the service provider
2. Work with the service provider to develop and deliver agreed Transformation Phase innovation deliverables
3. Establish a joint innovation culture with the service provider

Service provider recommendations include the following:

1. Agree and establish innovation governance with the client
2. Work with the client to develop and deliver agreed Transformation Phase innovation deliverables
3. Establish a joint innovation culture with the client

Client Recommendations

Recommendation One—Agree and establish innovation governance with your service provider

So, the service contract has been signed, what now? In terms of innovation, the first step is to establish an effective and practical approach for jointly governing innovation with your new service provider.

If a framework for this has been included in a contract schedule, this can be used as a guideline. In any case, key recommend activities include the following:

1. Confirm Innovation Sponsor(s) in the client organization
2. Appoint Innovation Leader in the client organization
3. Establish Operational Innovation Governance with the service provider
4. Establish Executive Innovation Governance with the service provider
5. Agree innovation target setting and measurement with the service provider
6. Agree approach for positively communicating successful innovation with the service provider

Confirm Innovation Sponsor(s) in the Client Organization

It is likely that the client sponsor(s) for innovation activity will have been agreed during the Engagement Phase. If this is the case, this should be formally confirmed with the service provider. If not, the client should identify and appoint one or more sponsors for innovation activity with the service provider.

The Innovation Sponsor(s) are typically executive-level personnel, with skin in the game by being in a position to benefit if joint innovation is successfully delivered and alternately be impacted if it is not. Their key inputs include attending regularly scheduled (typically quarterly or half-yearly) executive governance meetings and ad hoc requests for support and input. They review progress made, assist with removing blockages to progress, measure the value and benefits delivered, and set future focus areas for innovation activities. It is often useful to have one sponsor who is part of the client's retained team who works directly with the service provider and one wider business sponsor, with the ability to bring in support of the wider organization when needed.

It is recommended the client Innovation Sponsor(s) meet with its opposite number(s) in the client as soon as possible in the Transformation Phase to establish a working relationship and review objectives and approach for innovation.

A key enabler for success will be a strong working relationship with the Innovation Sponsor(s) in the service provider organization. The Innovation Sponsor(s) should look to establish a win-win approach.

Appoint Innovation Leader in the Client Organization

The client should identify and appoint a leader for innovation activity with the service provider. For the majority of service relationships, the Leaders will have another role. This is fine but it is important to ensure the client Innovation Leader, even if part time, is named and has "managing, developing, and delivering innovation" formally set as part of his or her role, responsibilities, and priorities and measured as part of his or her performance appraisals, reviews, and so on.

To be effective, the client Innovation Leaders needs to have a wide skill set (at times they will be facilitators, interpreters and project managers and many other things) and also have excellent networking skills and generally good contacts, reputation, and knowledge of their organization, or the ability to quickly get them.

A key enabler for success will be a strong working relationship with the Innovation Leader in the service provider organization. The Innovation Leaders should look to establish a win-win approach.

Establish Operational Innovation Governance

Operational governance should be managed and owned by the named client and service provider Innovation Leaders. The client Innovation Leaders should meet with their opposite number in the service provider as soon as practicable.

The Innovation Leaders should agree a structured process for joint innovation management and execution (as outlined in Part Three below) and the tools they will use to track items from idea, challenge, and opportunity identification, through to development and eventual delivery and benefits realization.

The Innovation Leaders should also agree with the Innovation Sponsors how they will report progress and how the joint innovation management process will interlock with wider program, project, change management, and governance processes in the client and service provider organizations.

The Innovation Leaders should establish regular operational meetings, for example, on a weekly or fortnightly basis to track progress. Additional people in both organizations may be invited to these meetings, depending on the context of the service relationship and agreed approach and scope of innovation activity.

It is assumed that innovation committed by the service provider to be delivered within the Transformation Phase change program will be managed as part of wider service relationship governance, rather than through innovation governance, although this may not always be the case.

During the Transformation Phase change program, there may be an understandable desire within both organizations to hold off from wider scope innovation activity to enable all focus on a successful Transformation. If this is the case, it is recommended that the Innovation Leaders spend some time agreeing focus areas for innovation during the Run Phase, including priority areas for service improvement and wider opportunities for innovation aligned to the client's business priorities. This will enable a fast start to ongoing innovation activities during the Run Phase.

Establish Executive Innovation Governance
with the Service Provider

The client Innovation Leader and client Innovation Sponsor(s) should agree an optimum approach for establishing Executive Innovation Governance and then review this with their opposite numbers in the service provider. The focus for Executive Innovation Governance should be reviewing progress, value, and benefits realized of existing innovation activities and setting future focus areas and priorities for innovation.

The Innovation Leaders and Sponsors should establish a schedule of regular Executive Innovation Governance meetings. Typically these take place on a quarterly or half-yearly basis but both the frequency and invitee list for these meetings will vary widely, depending on the context of the client–service provider relationship and agreed scope of joint innovation activities.

Typical Executive Innovation Governance activities include the following:

- Reviewing innovation activity progress
- Addressing major blockers to progress
- Measuring value and benefits realized of delivered innovation activities
- Setting focus areas and priorities for coming period
- Assisting positive communications and celebration of successfully delivered innovation activities

Typically, the Innovation Leaders will lead preparations for the Executive Innovation Governance meetings, including any premeeting stakeholder management activities, if these are required to ensure progress is made during the meeting and a successful outcome.

The meeting is intended to be an important part of, and integrated with, overall governance between client and service provider organizations. To be effective, the client and service provider Innovation Sponsors must attend the scheduled Executive Innovation Governance meetings and be empowered with decision-making capability.

Outside the window of the Executive Innovation Governance meetings, the Innovation Leaders will typically maintain close communications with the Sponsors and also contact them to help remove blockages to progress, review recommendations to progress innovation outside of agreed focus areas, and assist with other activities as required.

Agree Innovation Target Setting and Measurement
with the Service Provider

It is possible that the approach for setting targets for innovation and measuring impact will have been set in the Engagement Phase and included in a contract schedule. If this is the case, the client Innovation Leader and Sponsor(s) should review the details with their opposite number(s) in the service provider organization to ensure expectations are correctly set and a common level of understanding is in place across the organizations.

If not, then the targets and measurement approach for innovation should be agreed between the Innovation Sponsors, supported by the Innovation Leaders. The specific approach adopted will likely vary depending on the context of the service relationship and scope of innovation activities. To provide a level of guidance, a pragmatic approach has been documented below. This measures innovation in two ways.

The first measure is to focus measurement on the individual innovation items that progress beyond the Qualify Potential and Business Case step in the joint innovation management process funnel. Each of these must have a business case to move any further forward in the process. The business case will stand on hard measures such as cost savings, increase in revenue, customer retention, specific service key performance indicator measurements, and so on. All of these are clearly measurable and the "innovation" once delivered should be measured for the value delivered and benefits realized, both in absolute terms and against the business case. As these items have been generated and/or significantly accelerated by the focus on joint innovation, the benefits realized can be rightly attributed to joint innovation. Positive results can show the value of joint innovation and any negative results the opposite.

It is noted that this approach sets and measures the objectives and success of individual innovation activities and projects, rather than overall joint innovation activities. However, a small number of very positive returns through delivered innovation activities can soon become a very positive measure of the success of the overall joint focus on innovation.

The second measure is recommended for wider measurement of overall joint innovation between the client and service provider. This can be done in terms of typical Set-Met objectives and/or formal scores for Client Satisfaction for the client from the service provider, in terms of the benefits derived from joint innovation activities. Such measures do rely on an effective and honest relationship being in place between the client and service provider to work.

A subset of client and service providers may focus their innovation definition, scope, and focus areas into one specific thing. If this is the case, then an overall hard outcome-based objective and measure of success may be much easier to define. For example, if innovation is defined as "Use of new ideas to reduce the client's costs" and scope and focus areas of innovation are also specifically targeted onto cost, a cost-saving target could be agreed, which would be measurable. Equally, this would work for revenue generation, customer retention, customer service ratings, and so on. As always, it will depend on the context of the client–service provider relationship.

Typically the assessment of innovation achievement will be reviewed during Executive Innovation Governance meetings.

Agree approach for Positively Communicating Successful Innovation with the Service Provider

It is recommended the client Innovation Leader and Sponsor agree with their opposite numbers in the service provider how successfully delivered innovations will be positively communicated across both organizations and beyond. The overall innovation governance approach and plans for each innovation which progresses to the right hand side of the funnel should include a plan to positively communicate and jointly celebrate success. A further positive approach will be to target submission of successfully delivered innovations for internal and external awards.

Recommendation Two—Work with the service provider to develop and deliver agreed Transformation Phase innovation deliverables

If specific innovation activity has been agreed to be delivered as part of the Transformation Phase change program, the client will need to work with the service provider to ensure it is delivered. As the type, shape, and scope of potential innovation activity will vary wildly, it is not intended to make recommendations here, other than to remind the client that they need to take an active role in working with the service provider to ensure the innovation is delivered. Remember, in a service relationship innovation does not get done to the client, it is delivered for and with them.

Recommendation Three—Establish a joint innovation culture with your service provider

Chapter Seven includes a section on the importance of developing a joint innovation culture, with key elements including leadership and enabling support from the top, innovation from everyone, and the power of positive communications. One of the key recommendations for achieving successful joint innovation is to develop a positive culture for innovation where new ideas are encouraged, the best ones taken forward, and people behind ones which deliver real value rewarded, as success is celebrated. This should begin during the Transformation Phase of the relationship and be carried forward during the Run Phase.

There is so much which could be written here, perhaps a book in itself, but the initial recommendation for the client organization is for the Innovation Sponsor and Innovation Leader to include a set of activities, within their wider plans focused on engaging their own employees in innovation-related activities, where possible teaming, for example, in idea generation sessions, with teams in the service provider. Joint team awards and rewards for the best generated ideas and delivered innovations will foster partnership and a stronger overall relationship between the client and service provider teams. There is a little more detail behind wider scale potential joint innovation culture activities in Chapter Seven. One last point for now—this should not be a one-off activity but something which becomes an ongoing mantra through the life cycle of the relationship and runs as a theme across the full portfolio of your service providers.

Service Provider Recommendations

Recommendation One—Agree and establish innovation governance with your client

So, the service contract has been signed, what now? In terms of innovation, the first step is to establish an effective and practical approach for jointly governing innovation with your new client.

If a framework for this has been included in a contract schedule, this can be used as a guideline. In any case, key recommend activities include the following:

1. Confirm Innovation Sponsor(s) in the service provider organization
2. Appoint Innovation Leader in the service provider organization
3. Establish Operational Innovation Governance with the client
4. Establish Executive Innovation Governance with the client

5. Agree innovation target setting and measurement with the client
6. Agree approach for positively communicating successful innovation with the client

Confirm Innovation Sponsor(s) in the Service Provider Organization

The service provider sponsors for innovation activity may have been agreed during the Engagement Phase. If this is the case, this should be formally confirmed with the client. If not, the service provider should identify and appoint a sponsor for innovation activity with the client.

The Innovation Sponsors are typically executive-level personnel, with skin in the game by being in a position to benefit if joint innovation is successfully delivered and alternately be impacted if it is not. Their key inputs include attending regularly scheduled (typically quarterly or half-yearly) executive governance meetings and ad hoc requests for support and input. They review progress made, assist with removing blockages to progress, measure the value and benefits delivered, and set future focus areas for innovation activities. It is often useful to have one sponsor who is part of the service provider's client account team and one off-account sponsor, with the ability to bring in support of the wider organization when needed.

It is recommended the service provider Innovation Sponsors meet with their opposite numbers in the service provider as soon as possible in the Transformation Phase to establish a working relationship and review objectives and approach for innovation.

A key enabler for success will be a strong working relationship with the Innovation Sponsors in the client organization. The Innovation Sponsors should look to establish a win-win approach.

Appoint Innovation Leader in the Service Provider Organization

The service provider should identify and appoint a leader for innovation activity with the client. For the majority of service relationships, the Leaders will have another role. This is fine but it is important to ensure the service provider Innovation Leader, even if part time, is named and has "managing, developing, and delivering innovation" formally set as part of their role, responsibilities, and priorities and measured as part of their performance appraisals, reviews, and so on.

To be effective, the service provider Innovation Leader needs to have a wide skill set (at times they will be facilitators, interpreters, project managers, and so on) and also have excellent networking skills and generally good contacts, reputation, and knowledge of their organization, or the ability to quickly get them.

A key enabler for success will be a strong working relationship with the Innovation Leader in the client organization. The Innovation Leaders should look to establish a win-win approach.

Establish Operational Innovation Governance

Operational governance should be managed and owned by the named client and service provider Innovation Leaders. The service provider Innovation Leaders should meet with their opposite number in the client as soon as practicable.

The Innovation Leaders should agree a structured process for joint innovation management and execution (as outlined in Part Three below) and the tools they will use to track items from idea, challenge, and opportunity identification, through to development and eventual delivery and benefits realization.

The Innovation Leaders should also agree with the Innovation Sponsors how they will report progress and how the joint innovation management process will interlock with wider program, project, change management, and governance processes in the client and service provider organizations.

The Innovation Leaders should establish regular operational meetings, for example, on a weekly or fortnightly basis to track progress. Additional people in both organizations may be invited to these meetings, depending on the context of the service relationship and agreed approach and scope of innovation activity.

It is assumed that innovation committed by the service provider to be delivered within the Transformation Phase change program will be managed as part of wider service relationship governance, rather than through innovation governance, although this may not always be the case.

During the Transformation Phase change program, there may be an understandable desire within both organizations to hold off from wider scope innovation activity to enable all focus on a successful Transformation. If this is the case, it is recommended that the Innovation Leaders spend some time agreeing focus areas for innovation during the Run Phase, including priority areas for service improvement and wider opportunities for innovation aligned to the client's business priorities. This will enable a fast start to ongoing innovation activities during the Run Phase.

Establish Executive Innovation Governance with the Client

The service provider Innovation Leader and service provider Innovation Sponsors should agree an optimum approach for establishing Executive Innovation Governance and then review this with their opposite numbers in the client. The focus for Executive Innovation Governance should be reviewing progress, value, and benefits realized of existing innovation activities and setting future focus areas and priorities for innovation.

The Innovation Leaders and Sponsors should establish a schedule of regular Executive Innovation Governance meetings. Typically, these take place on a quarterly or half-yearly basis but both the frequency and invitee list for these meetings will vary widely, depending on the context of the client–service provider relationship and agreed scope of joint innovation activities.

Typical Executive Innovation Governance activities include the following:

- Reviewing innovation activity progress
- Addressing major blockers to progress
- Measuring value and benefits realized of delivered innovation activities
- Setting focus areas and priorities for coming period
- Assisting positive communications and celebration of successfully delivered innovation activities

Typically, the Innovation Leaders will lead preparations for the Executive Innovation Governance meetings, including any premeeting stakeholder management activities, if these are required to ensure progress is made during the meeting and a successful outcome.

The meeting is intended to be an important part of, and integrated with, overall governance between client and service provider organizations. To be effective, the client and service provider Innovation Sponsors must attend the scheduled Executive Innovation Governance meetings and be empowered with decision-making capability.

Outside the window of the Executive Innovation Governance meetings, the Innovation Leaders will typically maintain close communications with the Sponsors and also contact them to help remove blockages to progress, review recommendations to progress innovation outside of agreed focus areas, and assist with other activities as required.

Agree Innovation Target Setting and Measurement with the Client

It is possible that the approach for setting targets for innovation and measuring impact will have been set in the Engagement Phase and included in a contract schedule. If this is the case, the service provider Innovation Leader and Sponsors should review the details with their opposite numbers in the client organization to ensure expectations are correctly set and a common level of understanding.

If not, then the targets and measurement approach for innovation should be agreed between the Innovation Sponsors, supported by the Innovation Leaders. The specific approach adopted will likely vary depending on the context of the service relationship and scope of innovation activities. To provide a level of guidance, a pragmatic approach has been documented below. This measures innovation in two ways.

The first measure is to focus measurement on the individual innovation items which progress beyond the Qualify Potential and Business Case step in the joint innovation management process funnel. Each of these must have a business case to move any further forward in the process. The business case will stand on hard measures such as cost savings, increase in revenue, customer retention, specific service key performance indicator measurements, and so on. All of these are clearly measurable and the "innovation" once delivered should be measured for the value delivered and benefits realized, both in absolute terms and against the business case. As these items have been generated and/or significantly accelerated by the focus on joint innovation, the benefits realized can be rightly attributed to joint innovation. Positive results can show the value of joint innovation and any negative results the opposite.

It is noted that this approach sets and measures the objectives and success of individual innovation activities and projects, rather than over-all joint innovation activities. However, a small number of very positive returns through delivered innovation activities can soon become a very positive measure of the success of the overall joint focus on innovation.

The second measure is recommended for wider measurement of over-all joint innovation between the client and service provider. This can be done in terms of typical Set-Met objectives and/or formal scores for Client Satisfaction for the client from the service provider, in terms of the benefits derived from joint innovation activities. Such measures do rely on an effective and honest relationship being in place between the client and service provider to work.

A subset of client and service providers may focus their innovation definition, scope, and focus areas into one specific thing. If this is the case, then an overall hard outcome-based objective and measure of success may be much easier to define. For example, if innovation is defined as "Use of new ideas to reduce the client's costs" and scope and focus areas of innovation are also specifically targeted onto cost, a cost-saving target could be agreed, which would be measurable. Equally, this would work for revenue generation, customer retention, customer service ratings, and so on. As always, it will depend on the context of the client–service provider relationship.

Typically the assessment of innovation achievement will be reviewed during Executive Innovation Governance meetings.

Agree Approach for Positively Communicating Successful Innovation with the Client

It is recommended the service provider Innovation Leader and Sponsor agree with their opposite numbers in the client how successfully delivered innovations will be positively communicated across both organizations and beyond. The overall innovation governance approach and plans for each innovation which progresses to the right hand side of the funnel should include a plan to positively communicate and jointly celebrate success. A further positive approach will be to target submission of successfully delivered innovations for internal and external awards.

Recommendation Two—Work with the client to develop and deliver agreed Transformation Phase innovation deliverables

If specific innovation activity has been agreed to be delivered as part of the Transformation Phase change program, the client will need to work with the service provider to ensure it is delivered. As the type, shape, and scope of potential innovation activity will vary wildly, it is not intended to make recommendations here, other than to remind the service providers that they need to take an active role in working with the client to ensure the innovation is delivered. Remember, in a service relationship innovation does not get done to the client, it is delivered for and with them.

Recommendation Three—Establish a joint innovation culture with your service provider

Chapter Seven includes a section on the importance of developing a joint innovation culture, with key elements including leadership and enabling support from the top, innovation from everyone, and the power of positive communications. One of the key recommendations for achieving successful joint innovation is to develop a positive culture for innovation where new ideas are encouraged, the best ones taken forward, and people behind ones which deliver real value rewarded, as success is celebrated. This should begin during the Transformation Phase of the relationship and be carried forward during the Run Phase.

There is so much which could be written here, perhaps a book in itself, but the initial recommendation for the service provider organization is for the Innovation Sponsor and Innovation Leader to include a set of activities, within their wider plans focused on engaging their own employees in innovation-related activities, where possible teaming, for example, in idea generation sessions, with teams in the client. Joint team awards and rewards for the best generated ideas and delivered innovations will foster partnership and a stronger overall relationship between the client and service provider teams. There is a little more detail behind wider scale potential joint innovation culture activities in Chapter Seven. One last point for now—this should not be a one-off activity but something which becomes an ongoing mantra through the life cycle of the relationship and runs as a theme across the full portfolio of your clients.

Part Three—Run Phase for New Service Relationship

This section documents recommendations for client and service provider organizations during the Run Phase of a contract for a service relationship, with a focus on establishing and running a Joint Innovation Management and Execution process. It is also possible that the actions below will be carried out earlier, during the Transformation Phase of a service relationship. The section has been split into two subsections, one focused on the client and one focused on the service provider.

Client recommendations include the following:

1. Work with the service provider to develop and run a Joint Innovation Management and Execution process
2. Deliver quick-win innovations
3. Manage innovation governance with the service provider

Service provider recommendations include the following:

1. Work with the client to develop and run a Joint Innovation Management and Execution process
2. Deliver quick-win innovations
3. Manage innovation governance with the client

Chapter Five includes a detailed description of a framework for a Joint Innovation Management and Execution Process, with the focus on joint development and proactive management of a "process" to systematically move items forward from an initial idea, challenge or opportunity stage through to full implementation, and delivery of value and benefits realization.

The diagram below shows the key innovation activities in a deliberately simple five-step innovation management process.

Innovation Management and Execution

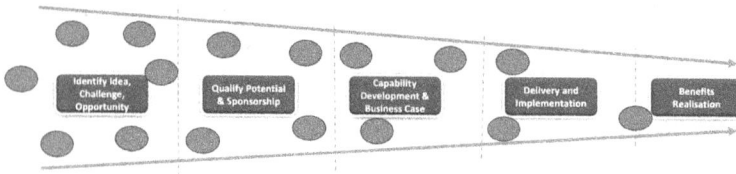

At a summary level, ideas, business challenges, and opportunities for innovation enter the funnel from the left. Typically, these are aligned to the agreed focus areas for joint innovation activity.

Selected items progress through the gated steps of the funnel. Although a relatively large number of items may enter the funnel, the intention is to use the initial steps to quickly identify those with the best sponsorship, business case, expected outcomes, and probability of success. The majority of resource intensive innovation development and delivery activities will then focus on a relatively small number of items, aligned with the client's business priorities and the service provider's ability to deliver value. These are progressed and exit the funnel on the right as delivered innovations, which are then tracked for their benefits realized.

Client Recommendations

Recommendation One—Work with the service provider to develop and run a Joint Innovation Management and Execution process

A recommended framework for a Joint Innovation Management and Execution Process between a client and service provider is detailed in Chapter Five. To prevent whole scale duplication of the content of Chapter Five, full details of the process steps are not repeated here but the five steps of the process are summarized below:

- **Develop Innovation**—including client and service provider activities to:
  1. Identify ideas, challenges, and opportunities for applying innovation

2. Qualify potential and sponsorship for selected innovation activities

3. Develop capability and business case for selected innovation activities

- **Deliver Innovation**—including client and service provider activities to:

   1. Implement and deliver selected innovations to enable value to be derived

   2. Realize benefits of innovations delivered

It is strongly recommended that the client Innovation Leaders work with their opposite numbers in the service provider to set up a managed and gated process, such as the one described in Chapter Five, with items only entering the funnel when mutually agreed by both the client and service provider Innovation Leader.

It should be noted that the above is an example process. This should be reviewed and potentially tailored to fit best with the context of the client's organization and the relationship with the service provider.

As a first step, it is recommended the client team review how such a process will best integrate into its wider environment. Specifically, it is recommended that the client Innovation Leader agrees with the client Innovation Sponsor(s) how such a process will best work in the context of its own organization and their relationship with one or more service providers.

Specific factors for consideration include the following:

- Interlock with existing innovation management processes used across the client organization; if a successful innovation management process is already in place across the organization and/or the specific business unit, the recommendation would be to adopt this. The client Innovation Leader should agree with the client's wider innovation function how this will be managed and agree with the service provider which ideas and innovation items should enter the wider process and how they will be jointly managed and developed.

- Interlock with existing program, project, and change processes in the client organization—for example, the client–service provider innovation management process could be used to fast track selected ideas and innovation items into the later stages of these processes, such as at the Delivery and Implementation stage.

- Approach for managing innovation activities across multiple service providers—for example, the client may adopt one standard innovation management process for joint innovation with a number of service providers, with the client Innovation Leader managing idea selection and innovation development and delivery across the portfolio of service providers. The client Innovation Leader will select items to be developed in partnership with each specific service provider, based upon the strengths and capabilities of the service providers.

- Treatment of service improvement—a decision is needed whether the innovation management process will be used for incremental service improvement innovations or whether these should be managed via a different process.

- Interlock with wider management and governance of the client–service provider relationship, including inputs and outputs between innovation governance and wider governance.

Once the client Innovation Leader has agreed an optimum approach with his or her own organization, it is recommended that he or she engages with the service provider Innovation Leader to establish and document the process which will be used. This will need to take into account additional inputs from the service provider. For example, the service provider may have its own framework and/or excellent working examples of Innovation Management and Execution processes used with other clients, elements of which the client organization may wish to reuse.

The client Innovation Leader should also agree with the service provider Innovation Leader the reporting mechanisms to be used to communicate current state activity and progress. If possible, these reports should be made widely available and be very visible so that joint innovation activity can be monitored and progress positively and widely communicated.

The outcome of this work should be an agreed and documented joint Innovation Management and Execution Process, along with agreed reporting mechanisms.

Recommendation Two—Deliver Quick-Win Innovations

Once the joint Innovation Management and Execution Process is agreed, the real work starts. This is all about identifying ideas, challenges, and opportunities to enter into the funnel, and then developing and delivering them.

As Chapter Five describes this process in some detail, including walking through a successful real-life example, this level of detail is not repeated here. Instead, the recommendation is to ensure some of the initial innovation items selected to enter the funnel are "quick win" opportunities. These should be items which the client and service provider Innovation Leaders, supported by their Innovation Sponsors, believe can be progressed relatively quickly through the steps of the funnel to deliver early benefits and demonstrate the value of a focus on joint innovation. This can also be highly positive for the wider client and service provider relationship, as a means of demonstrating the additional value for the client from the relationship over and above the benefits of the core services provided.

The client Innovation Leader should engage with the service provider Innovation Leader to identify potential quick wins, aligned to the business priorities for the client and agreed focus areas for innovation. The client Innovation Leaders may have a number of ideas already identified in the client organization which they wish to pursue.

Another approach is to run joint innovation workshops, focused on generating ideas for quick wins, with key stakeholders from the client and service provider organizations. Equally, similar sessions can be run using online idea generation, to enable wider multisite and multicountry inputs. As detailed in Chapter Five, the preparation, execution, and follow-up for these sessions will be a critical determinant for success.

These innovation events should combine the client and industry-specific knowledge and expertise of the client organization with the domain expertise, industry, and potentially cross-industry knowledge and expertise of the service provider organization. The events should be positively communicated and participation from client and service provider teams encouraged, as this is effectively part of developing a joint innovation culture.

However the quick win ideas are generated, a small number should be selected for fast track development and confirmation of capability and business case and progressed rapidly through the joint Innovation Management and Execution process. The earlier benefits can be realized, confirmed, and positively communicated the better.

Recommendation Three—*Manage innovation governance with the service provider*

Once an active flow of ideas, challenges, and opportunities begins to flow into the left hand side of the joint Innovation Management and Execution Process funnel, the process will need to be governed. The Innovation Leaders will need to lead Operational and Executive Innovation Governance activities, working with their Innovation Sponsors, identified sponsor(s) for specific innovation initiatives and wider stakeholders. Further details of the key activities required to manage Operational and Executive Innovation governance are detailed in Chapter Five.

The client Innovation Leader needs to hold the service provider to account to ensure it suitably participate in, proactively support, and where necessary fund innovation activities. It is recommended the client Innovation Leaders does this in a way which balances the needs of their organization as their primary driver with the knowledge that to be successful there needs to be a benefit from the innovation activity for the service provider also. If this is not considered, there is a risk the service provider will lose interest and motivation in supporting future innovation activities. The most obvious benefit for the service provider will be increased business but the client Innovation Leader should also consider how innovation activity can deliver other benefits to the service provider. These could include retention of existing business, increased client satisfaction ratings, client references, and external awards, all of which have a tangible value to service provider organizations.

Service Provider Recommendations

Recommendation One—*Work with the client to develop and run a Joint Innovation Management and Execution process*

A recommended framework for a Joint Innovation Management and Execution Process between a client and service provider is detailed in Chapter Five. To prevent whole scale duplication of the content of Chapter Five, full details of the process steps are not repeated here but the five steps of the process are summarized below:

- **Develop Innovation**—including client and service provider activities to:
    1. Identify ideas, challenges, and opportunities for applying innovation
    2. Qualify potential and sponsorship for selected innovation activities
    3. Develop capability and business case for selected innovation activities
- **Deliver Innovation**—including client and service provider activities to
    1. Implement and deliver selected innovations to enable value to be derived
    2. Realize benefits of innovations delivered

It is strongly recommended that the service provider Innovation Leaders work with their opposite number in the client to set up a managed and gated process, such as the one described in Chapter Five, with items only entering the funnel when mutually agreed by both the client and service provider Innovation Leader.

It should be noted that the above is an example process. This should be reviewed and potentially tailored to fit best with the context of the client's organization and the relationship with the service provider.

While the client team will be reviewing how such a process will best fit into its wider environment, it is recommended the service provider Innovation Leader works with their own organization to identify key inputs for getting the right joint Innovation Management and Execution process in place.

Specific factors for consideration include the following:

- Intellectual capital within the wider service provider organization covering successful innovation management processes and approaches.
- Examples of successful innovation management processes and approaches used with other clients.

- Approach for managing innovation activities across multiple service providers—if applicable, the service provider will need to develop an approach for how they will work with other service providers, potentially including direct competitors, on innovation activities.
- Treatment of service improvement—a decision is needed whether the innovation management process will be used for incremental service improvement innovations or whether these should be managed via a different process.
- Interlock with wider management and governance of the client–service provider relationship, including inputs and outputs between innovation governance and wider governance.

Once the service provider Innovation Leader has agreed an optimum approach with their own organization, it is recommended they engage with the client Innovation Leader to establish and document the process which will be used. This will need to take into accounts additional inputs from the client. For example, the client may have existing innovation management processes and interlocks will be needed with existing programmer, project and change processes in the client organization.

The service provider Innovation Leader should also agree with the client Innovation Leader the reporting mechanisms to be used to communicate current state activity and progress. If possible, these reports should be made widely available and be very visible, so that joint innovation activity can be monitored and progress positively and widely communicated.

The outcome of this work should be an agreed and documented joint Innovation Management and Execution Process, along with agreed reporting mechanisms.

Recommendation Two—Deliver Quick Win Innovations

Once the joint Innovation Management and Execution Process is agreed, the real work starts. This is all about identifying ideas, challenges and opportunities to enter into the funnel, and then developing and delivering them.

As Chapter Five describes this process in some detail, including walking through a successful real life example, this level of detail is not repeated here. Instead, the recommendation is to ensure some of the initial innovation items selected to enter the funnel are "quick win" opportunities, which the client and service provider Innovation Leaders, supported by their Innovation Sponsor(s), believe can be progressed relatively quickly through the steps of the funnel to deliver early benefits and demonstrate the value of a focus on joint innovation. This can also be highly positive for the wider client and service provider relationship, as a means of demonstrating the additional value for the client from the relationship over and above the benefits of the core services provided.

The service provider Innovation Leader should engage with the client Innovation Leader to identify potential quick wins, aligned to the business priorities for the client and agreed focus areas for innovation. The service provider Innovation Leader may have a number of ideas already identified in the service provider organization which they wish to pursue, for example ideas from innovations successfully delivered with other clients, where the intellectual property is not protected or is owned by the service provider.

Another approach is to run joint innovation workshops, focused on generating ideas for quick wins, with key stakeholders from the client and service provider organizations. Equally, similar session can be run using online idea generation, to enable wider multisite and multicountry inputs. As detailed in Chapter Five the preparation, execution and follow-up for these sessions will be a critical determinant for success.

These innovation events should combine the client and industry specific knowledge and expertise of the client organization with the domain expertise, industry and potentially cross-industry knowledge and expertise of the service provider organization. The events should be positively communicated and participation from client and service provider teams encouraged, as this is effectively part of developing a joint innovation culture.

However the quick win ideas are generated, a small number should be selected for fast track development and confirmation of capability and business case and progressed rapidly through the joint Innovation Management and Execution process. The earlier benefits can be realized, confirmed and positively communicated the better.

Recommendation Three—Manage innovation governance with the client

Once an active flow of ideas, challenges and opportunities begins to flow into the left hand side of the joint Innovation Management and Execution Process funnel, the client and service provider Innovation Leaders will need to manage Operational and Executive Innovation Governance, working with the Innovation Sponsor for overall innovation activities within the client–service provider relationship, identified sponsor(s) for specific innovation initiatives and wider stakeholders. Further details of the key activities required to manage Operational and Executive Innovation governance are detailed in Chapter Five.

The service provider Innovation Leader needs to ensure the client suitably participates in, proactively supports and where necessary funds innovation activities. It is recommended the service provider Innovation Leader does this in a way which balances the needs of their organization with the knowledge that to be successful there needs to be a benefit from the innovation activity for the client. If this is not considered, it is likely the client will lose interest and motivation in supporting future innovation activities. The most obvious benefit areas for the client will be linked to their business priorities, which should be driving the selected focus areas for innovation These could include increasing revenue, reducing cost, gaining additional customers, retaining existing customers and so on, all of which have a tangible value to client organizations.

Part Four—Run Phase for Existing Service Relationship

This section documents recommendations for client and service provider organizations during the Run Phase of a service contract for an established service relationship, which to date either hasn't had a focus on innovation or if there has been a focus, it has not been successful. The section has been split into two subsections, one focused on each of these two scenarios.

Kick-Off Joint Innovation

This section focuses on a scenario where a client and service provider have implemented a successful relationship focused on delivery of a core service but to date have not included a focus on innovation. The initial desire for change can come from multiple angles—pull from the client and/or push from the service provider.

Recommendation One—Review Motivations

The client may be happy with the core service but desire future improvements. For example, the client may have concerns that the service, although currently meeting their needs, is not evolving to match their changing needs for the future and/or may be happy with the service provider's core service and their focus on ongoing service improvement innovation (noting, as always, not all clients consider service improvement to be innovation) but believe they can achieve additional value from the relationship by leveraging the service provider's wider cross-industry, industry specific and/or specialist capabilities.

The service provider may be looking to drive innovation into the service to introduce their latest improvements and capabilities and potentially align the client's service with their wider client portfolio to achieve economies of scale and/or recognize innovation provides a potential avenue to develop opportunities to grow their own revenue and business with the client.

Whether the desire to expand the relationship to focus on innovation comes from a pull from the client or a push from the service provider, both parties will need to agree this is something they wish to do and are prepared to proactively support moving forward. If the client simply wishes the service provider to invest with no potential return or expects the service provider to deliver innovation to them, whilst providing no input themselves, innovation will not work. Equally, if the service provider considers innovation as being all about attempting to sell more stuff to the client, without properly understanding the needs of and the business value for the client, they will fail. Innovation in a service relationship is a two way street. The client and service provider need to both put something in for both to expect to get something out. Lecture over.

I have often talked to client and service provider teams about the importance of the "Step Zero" for establishing successful joint innovation. This is about getting the basics right. The core service needs to be delivering and the relationship needs to be in a positive place. Without these basics, innovation will not thrive but if they are in place, the client and service provider are in an excellent position to begin their joint focus on developing and delivering innovation together.

Recommendation Two—Develop Joint Innovation as if in a New Relationship

In terms of what is needed to get this working, the recommendation is to work through the recommendations in sequence as described in Parts One, Two and Three of this chapter. Although these Parts are written with a new client–service provider relationship in mind, they will be equally effective when used in an existing relationship, once the "Step Zero" basics are in place.

The activity should begin with the client taking a step back to understand what innovation really means to them in the context of the service relationship and what they want from it. The client should engage positively with the service provider and both parties should agree sponsors and leaders for innovation activity, establish a governance framework and a practical innovation management and execution process, which they should initially populate with quick win innovation opportunities. The outcome of these should be positive populated and a range of actions undertaken to develop and maintain a positive joint innovation culture across the two organizations.

The two parties will face challenges. For example agreement of funding mechanisms for early stage innovation activity is a typical sticking point. But none of these challenges should be insurmountable, as long as both parties are really committed to ensuring innovation is delivered in the context of their service relationship, in a manner which delivers real additional value and benefits to the client's business and there is something in it for the service provider.

Fix Joint Innovation

This section focuses on a scenario where a client and service provider have attempted to develop and deliver joint innovation in the context of their service relationship but to date have not achieved a successful outcome. This can be due to a myriad of reasons. Many of these are outlined in the client and service provider challenges outlined in Chapters Two and Three. The example of Failed Joint Innovation Activity in Chapter Six highlights an amalgamation of a number of real life examples.

Recommendation One—Take a Step Back

When innovation has been attempted but is not working, the recommendation is for both organizations to take a step back and honestly reflect not just on what they believe the other party has done wrong but also where they themselves may have failed. Once again, I believe use of Design Thinking techniques and approaches can have a huge impact here. A key part of this step back should be about empathy and understanding the position of your opposite numbers in the client or service provider team. If joint innovation is going to succeed, it will need to be developed and delivered together and the relationship will need to proceed on a win-win basis, rather than us and them. If it has failed to date. it is likely to be because both parties have failed to some degree. In this period of reflection, both parties should attempt to understand where they believe their own organization went wrong, as well as where their partner went wrong, along with what needs to be changed to enable joint success. This will require a level of honesty, maturity and to some degree, openness, from both parties.

Both parties will also be very dependent on "Step Zero" for establishing joint client–service provider innovation—getting the basics right. If the core service is not delivering and/or the overall relationship is not in a positive place, joint innovation will not thrive.

Recommendation Two—Begin Again—Develop Joint Innovation as if in a New Relationship

If the basics are in place and both parties have taken a step back, the recommendation is to work through the recommendations in sequence of Parts One, Two and Three of this chapter. Although these Parts are written with a new client–service provider relationship in mind, they will be equally effective when used in an existing relationship, once the "Step Zero" basics are in place.

The activity should begin with the client holding a review to understand what innovation really means to them in the context of the service relationship and what they want from it. The client should engage positively with the service provider and both parties should agree sponsors and leaders for innovation activity, establish a governance framework and a practical innovation management and execution process, which they should initially populate with quick win innovation opportunities. The outcome of these should be positive populated and a range of actions undertaken to develop and maintain a positive joint innovation culture across the two organizations.

At each step along the way, the client and service provider should place special emphasis on ensuring they address the areas where one or both parties acknowledge they went wrong the first time around.

The two parties will face challenges. For example, due to the failed history to date, the wider employee base in both client and service provider, may have lost faith in the ability of one or both parties to deliver innovation. Here, the emphasis should be on fast development, delivery and positive communication of quick wins and concerted progress on developing a tangible innovation culture. To win over a skeptical employee base, these activities will be even more important than with a new relationship or when first launching joint innovation activities in an existing relationship.

CHAPTER 9

Final Conclusions

In Summary

In summary, achieving innovation *by design* in a service relationship is not just possible but wholly achievable, although at times it may not be easy. The Step Zero basics of solid service delivery and positive relationship must be in place. It will require thinking, input, and effort above and beyond business as usual related activities by both the client and service provider organizations, but get it right, and the potential rewards for both the client and service provider will be significant.

Both parties will need to work collaboratively together to put in place Innovation Governance and a practical and, at times, pragmatic Innovation Management and Execution process, which works well, integrates with wider activities in the client, and taps into the full depth and breadth of capabilities within the service provider. The diagram shown below highlights the major activity areas required for joint innovation *by design*.

Mapping to the Innovation Management Process

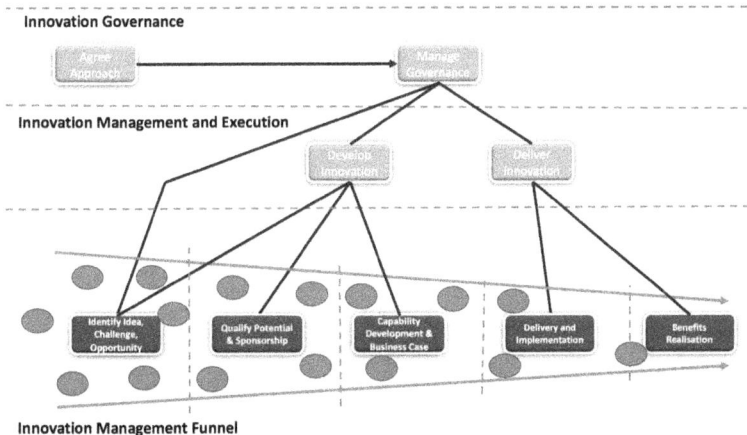

In common with innovation within a single organization, the following key enablers must be in place:

- Executive sponsorship and proactive support for making innovation happen
- Innovation leaders/managers (albeit perhaps part time) with T- or TT-shaped skill sets and the responsibility for ensuring innovation is managed, developed, and delivered
- An effective, practical, and pragmatic innovation management and execution process to take in ideas, challenges, and opportunities, develop the capability and business case of the best ideas and innovations, and see them through to delivery and benefits realization
- An effective governance mechanism for innovation to set priorities and targets, review progress, remove blockages, measure the value of innovation delivered, and positively communicate the innovation success
- One or more agreed funding mechanisms for the early stages of innovation development to fund activity until the capability and business case are solid enough for standard business investment
- The ability to hire, develop, and nurture the next generations of employees to bring in new thinking, while retaining and tapping into the experience and knowledge base of existing employees—blending the two together to create new and differentiating ideas and capabilities
- An innovation culture across and beyond the two organizations, supported at an executive and operational level, where developing ideas and opportunities is part of everybody's job and not limited to a research and development organization or an appointed innovation leader
- A focus on open innovation for looking beyond the organization for the best ideas and opportunities

To achieve success, the service provider, in particular, must do the following:

- Build an innovation management, development, and delivery capability in the organization that spans across client accounts and supports and enables innovation at a client account level

- Get the Step Zero basics right—deliver a solid core service and maintain a positive relationship with the client
- Be proactive—find out what innovation means to the client, what the client's business priorities for innovation are, and then focus joint innovation activities in these areas
- Leverage capabilities from across the wider organization to develop and deliver innovation with the client
- Build an innovation culture in employees and partners, which spans into the client organization

To achieve success, the client, in particular, must do the following:

- Begin thinking and planning about innovation even in Pre-Engagement Phase planning activities and carry this through during Engagement, Transformation, and Run Phases of the life cycle—if the client knows what it wants, it will be much easier for the service provider to deliver it and for the client to tell they're getting it (or not getting it)
- Get the Step Zero basics right—enable a solid core service and maintain a positive relationship with the service provider
- Be proactive—understand what innovation means in the context of the service and service provider relationship, what the business priorities for innovation are, clearly articulate this to the service provider, and then focus joint innovation activities in these areas
- Reach out across the wider client organization to understand where the service provider could deliver additional value through innovation
- Build an innovation culture in employees and partners, which spans into the service provider organization and across the portfolio of service providers

As detailed in Chapter Eight, the best approach will be to embed innovation into the relationship from the very beginning, from Pre-Engagement Planning and Engagement, through Transformation and into Run phases. However, innovation can be introduced as a mechanism for driving additional client value with benefits for the service provider at any time during a service relationship. Even if it fails, it can be recovered and relaunched if . . . both parties are willing to work together, acknowledge their own failings, and focus on achieving innovation *by design* together as they move forward.

I'd like to finish on a point, learned through experience, as recommended to me by a C-level executive from a very large global organization. Don't be shy to shout about your success. If the joint team delivers a significant innovation, which delivers real value for the client's business, whether a service improvement, a Transformation change, or a wider scope innovation, positively communicate and celebrate the value and the joint success. Enter it for internal and external awards and watch the snowball effect. People love being linked to, being part of, inputting, and working with a successful innovation program.

Done right, innovation is not just an executive slogan or buzzword, it is about applying new ideas, or existing ideas in new ways, to result in change that delivers value—and in a service relationship the value and benefits will be for both the client and the service provider.

Index

OTHER TITLES IN OUR SERVICE SYSTEMS AND INNOVATIONS IN BUSINESS AND SOCIETY COLLECTION

Jim Spohrer, IBM and Haluk Demirkan, Arizona State University, *Editors*

- *Sustainable Service* by Adi Wolfson
- *Fair Pay: Adaptively Win-Win Customer Relationships* by Richard Reisman
- *Business Engineering and Service Design, Second Edition* by Oscar Barros
- *Service Design with Applications to Health Care Institutions* by Oscar Barros
- *Service Innovation* by Anders Gustafsson, Per Kristensson, Gary R. Schirr, and Lars Witell
- *Matching Services to Markets: The Role of the Human Sensorium in Shaping Service-Intensive Markets* by H.B. Casanova
- *Achieving Success through Innovation: Cases and Insights from the Hospitality, Travel, and Tourism Industry* by Glenn Withiam
- *Designing Service Processes to Unlock Value, Second Edition* by Joy M. Field
- *Citizen-Centered Cities, Volume I: Case Studies of Public Involvement* by Paul R. Messinger

Announcing the Business Expert Press Digital Library

Concise e-books business students need for classroom and research

This book can also be purchased in an e-book collection by your library as

- a one-time purchase,
- that is owned forever,
- allows for simultaneous readers,
- has no restrictions on printing, and
- can be downloaded as PDFs from within the library community.

Our digital library collections are a great solution to beat the rising cost of textbooks. E-books can be loaded into their course management systems or onto students' e-book readers. The **Business Expert Press** digital libraries are very affordable, with no obligation to buy in future years. For more information, please visit **www.businessexpertpress.com/librarians**. To set up a trial in the United States, please email **sales@businessexpertpress.com**.

www.ingramcontent.com/pod-product-compliance
Lightning Source LLC
Chambersburg PA
CBHW071839200326
41519CB00016B/4174